THEY CAME...
THEY SAW...
THEY CONQUERED

Because of its strategic position between Europe, Africa and America, Gran Canaria has found itself at the centre of events involving some of the most notorious characters in European history.

Christopher Columbus (1451–1506)

Columbus, or Cristobal Colón to the Spaniards, was born in Italy, but it was the Spanish monarchs Ferdinand and Isabella who sponsored his attempt to discover a western sea route to India in 1492.

Setting out from Spain in the caravel *Santa María*, he called in at the Canary Islands, at that time the last port of call in the known world. His log book speaks of putting in at Las Palmas for repairs, though some historians maintain that although he sent his boat to Las Palmas he himself never set foot on Gran Canaria, preferring instead to stay on La Gomera where he was having an affair with the beautiful widow Countess Beatriz de Bobadilla.

On his first voyage to the New World, Columbus discovered Cuba and Hispaniola (Haiti) and returned in

The monument to Christopher Columbus in Alameda de Colón, Las Palmas

Sir Francis Drake (c1540-1596)

One person who conspicuously failed to conquer was the British seaman and buccaneer Sir Francis Drake, who launched an unsuccessful attack on Las Palmas in 1595. After his victory over the Spanish Armada in 1588, he continued his expeditions against the Spanish, which had earlier brought him great wealth from his capture of tobacco, sugar, spices and slaves. Driven back from Las Palmas, he sailed to the Caribbean, where he died of dysentery and was buried at sea. His defeat at Las Palmas is commemorated every year on 6 October with a festival on the peninsula of La Isleta.

triumph to the Spanish court. It is likely that he also called in at Las Palmas and stayed at what is now the Casa de Colón (► 63) during his third and fourth voyages to America which took place between 1498 and 1504.

Francisco Franco (1892–1975)

The military revolt which ushered in the Spanish Civil War (1936–1939) and the long period of dictatorship which followed had its roots in the Canary Islands. The Popular Front government elected in Madrid in 1936 had feared an uprising from right-wing generals and had dispatched them to far-flung outposts of Spain. Among them was General Franco, who was posted to Tenerife. He and his fellow conspirators hatched a plot to overthrow the régime and the commander of the Las Palmas garrison was shot dead in suspicious circumstances. Franco came over from Tenerife for the funeral, and a British plane which had been chartered from Croydon, ostensibly by a group of holidaymakers, flew him out of Gando, the only airfield in the Canaries, to take charge of the élite Spanish African army in Melilla, a Spanish enclave situated on the north coast of Morocco. Franco spent his final night in Las Palmas at the Hotel Madrid and announced his rebellion from the military headquarters in Parque San Telmo (► 67). The rest, as they say, is history.

General Franco led Spain for 36 years

On 16 December, 1965, more than a thousand guests travelled down from Las Palmas to witness the opening of the first hotel on the south coast. The Hotel Folias in San Agustín had 80 rooms and the price of a double room was just 500 pesetas.

It all began on Playa de las Canteras

Paradise

Tourists had already been visiting Gran Canaria for more than a century, and early travellers such as Briton A Samler Brown had written about the health benefits of the island's year-round spring climate. Until the 1960s, however, the only tourist resort on Gran Canaria was Playa de las Canteras in Las Palmas (➤ 70) and Maspalomas was little more than a desert. Nobody could have imagined that within a generation it would be turned into a vast holiday complex welcoming some three million foreign visitors a year.

Since the Spanish Conquest in 1478, Gran Canaria has tended to rely on a single cash crop as its main source of income. Sugar, wine, cochineal (a natural dye produced by insects feeding

Rural tourism is attracting walkers to the island (below and right)

island?

on the prickly pear plant) and bananas have all had their day, and the latest monoculture is tourism. Nobody doubts that the island is totally dependent on tourism – it provides almost 80 per cent of the gross domestic product – but people are starting to ask what can make it sustainable.

The first charter plane arrived from Düsseldorf in Germany in 1956, just as the

Good Advice
"Rheumatism, neuralgia, gout, scrofula, venereal and other diseases find the climate most suitable...if strength permits, excursions should frequently be made to the hills or to the mountains, the change of air, even if only for a few hours, being of great advantage. All hotels will provide luncheon in a basket."

A Samler Brown, *Madeira, Canary Islands and Azores: A Practical and Complete Guide for the use of Tourists and Invalids* (1889)

Franco government was beginning to market the Spanish costas as an attractive setting for a sun-and-sand holiday. Mallorca and the Costa Brava led the way, but the Canaries soon followed.

The first "urbanisations" on Gran Canaria were pioneered by Alejandro del Castillo, Conde de la Vega Grande, who was quick to spot the potential of his vast country estates in the south. By 1974, when Gando Airport opened, Playa del Inglés (➤ 129) had been built on the Maspalomas sand dunes and Gran Canaria was receiving almost a million tourists a year, drawn by the promise of golden sands and sunny skies.

Village houses, like this one in Agüimes, are now available for rent...

The island quickly established a reputation for cheap-and-cheerful package tourism which has proved hard to shake off.

At the same time, in spite of the economic benefits, tourism brought its problems, with areas of natural beauty

...but most people still stay in seaside apartments

threatened by potential pollution and overdevelopment. The population of inland villages began to dwindle as young people moved to the coast in search of work.

At the end of the 20th century, a serious debate began in Gran Canaria about the future of tourism on the island. The buzzwords today are "rural" and "quality", as Gran Canaria seeks to attract a new kind of visitor, interested in culture and history as well as sun, sea and sand.

Grants are being used to fund rural tourism projects, from the renovation of cave houses to the restoration of the *caminos reales* (royal

European grants are reviving the mountain areas (left and below)

paths). The newest resorts offer conference centres, golf courses, marinas and luxury hotels. Environmental initiatives such as the desalination of sea water and the recycling of water at golf courses and hotels are also helping to reduce problems.

The challenge of the 21st century is to continue to attract more tourists without upsetting the delicate balance of a fragile environment and a small island culture.

Veneguera

The arguments which raged throughout the 1990s over the remote beach of Veneguera (► 143) symbolised the ongoing battle between get-rich-quick developers and ecologists determined to preserve the last unspoiled corners of the island. Although Veneguera was eventually sold for development, it remains the westernmost limit of mass tourism on the south coast.

Gran Canaria in 2010?
- Five million visitors a year
- New resorts at Tauro, Playa de los Amadores and Veneguera
- GC1 motorway extended to Puerto Rico and Puerto de Mogán
- A second runway at Gando Airport, and possibly a new airport on the west coast

Cavemen
of the
Canaries

First Impressions

What did the Spanish conquerors find when they arrived on Gran Canaria in the 15th century?

They found a people who had never seen a wheel, had no knowledge of metals, and despite the fact that their ancestors had probably arrived from Africa by boat, did not appear to know how to sail. A people who were living in harmony with nature, totally untouched by the wars, the scientific discoveries and the artistic movements of medieval Europe. A people who made their homes in Stone Age villages of cave houses, yet with a degree of technical knowledge and social organisation that many "advanced" societies of today would envy.

"They kept lard and fat in earthenware jars, and fragrant woods for the needs of the dead; anointing them, smoking them and putting them into burnt sand... after 15 or 20 days, they placed them in the caves, if they were of the nobility; the rest they put in wasteland or lava rocks, making a hollow among the rocks and then covering them with mounds of stones."

Gómez Escudero
chronicler of the Spanish Conquest (1494)

The Guanches used poles to vault down the steep hillsides

Guanche Lifestyle

So what was life like for these aboriginal cavemen, who have come to be known as the Guanches? From the accounts of the early invaders, we know that they were exceptionally tall and fair-haired, traits which can still be seen in many Canarios today. They lived either in natural caves or in artificial cave dwellings which they carved out of the rock using primitive tools of stone or bone.

They grew barley and wheat, which they toasted and ground to make *gofio* (a type of flour) and also ate wild berries and figs. Goats, sheep and pigs were reared for milk, meat and hide, and fish and shellfish were gathered using nets. They wove baskets out of palm leaves, made simple red ochre pottery, and carved wood into plates, mugs, jewellery, weapons, doors and coffins.

Wrestling (► 25) and stick-fighting contests were organised, both for duels and as entertainment.

When people were wounded in battle they treated their injuries by trepanation (a surgical operation to the skull) or drew blood using

Cuatro Puertas means "four doors" in Spanish

a flintstone and made purgatives out of thistles.

Guanche Society

Guanche society was strictly feudal in nature, with clear social divisions between the nobles and the peasantry, who were easily distinguished by their shaven heads.

Gran Canaria was divided into two kingdoms, based at Telde (► 95) and Gáldar (► 98), each ruled by a *guanarteme* (king). Next down from the king, the most powerful figure was the *faycán* (viceroy), who acted as judge and

Cuatro Puertas, near Telde, was a sacred Guanche site

Below: Grain was stored at Cenboio de Valerón

high priest. The nobles would meet under a dragon tree or in a *tagoror* (assembly house) to take decisions affecting the community.

Grain was stored in communal granaries such as Cenobio de Valerón (➤ 90), and tithes were imposed on every citizen so that surplus grain could be reserved for periods of drought. The system of justice included execution by hanging or by dropping a large boulder onto the head, with lesser crimes punishable by the principle of "an eye for an eye".

Although they had no contact with any other society, many of the ideas developed by the Guanches were in the mainstream of European democratic thought.

Guanche Religion

Religion centred on Alcorán, the Supreme Creator, who was closely identified with sun, rain, mountains and the fertility of the earth. The Guanches also worshipped idols, many representing the female figure, such as those which can be

Modern-day cave homes in the Barranco de Guayadeque

seen at the Museo Canario in Las Palmas (➤ 56).

Religious ceremonies were sometimes carried out by the *harimaguadas* (vestal virgins), nuns who were confined to a convent for life. Other young

Mummies are on display in the Museo Canario in Las Palmas

women would be sent to the convent and fed a rich diet in preparation for marriage and childbirth, for which wide hips were considered essential requirements.

The most remarkable feature of Guanche spirituality was their practice of mummifying their dead, which has led to speculation that the Guanches were descended from the ancient Egyptians. As in many societies, the men who carried out this practice were treated as outsiders and excluded from the life of the community.

Cave-dwelling Today

Some of the cave houses in Gran Canaria have continued to be occupied right up to the present day by people seeking an alternative lifestyle or by villagers who appreciate the fact that they are cooler in summer and warmer in winter than conventional homes. The cavemen who originally inhabited them probably wouldn't recognise them today, however, with their additional telephones and satellite dishes. The best places for seeing cave houses

Aboriginal World
For more insight into the lives of the Guanches, visit the Museo Canario in Las Palmas (► 56) or Mundo Aborigen (► 140).

are Artenara (► 108) and La Atalaya (► 83), the suburbs of Telde (► 95) and the Barranco de Guayadeque (► 126).

You can learn about the lives of the Guanches on a visit to Mundo Aborigen, in the Barranco de Fataga

The Death of the Guanches

When Juan Rejón landed at Las Palmas in 1478, Gran Canaria was ruled by two Guanche kings. The *guanarteme* of Telde, Doramas, resisted the Spanish invasion and was killed at Arucas in 1481. Tenesor Samidan, king of Gáldar, was captured, converted to Christianity and taken to Spain. He returned to Gran Canaria in 1483 as Don Fernando Guanarteme in an effort to persuade his people to surrender before the Spaniards' final assault. Many did so, but others retreated to their stronghold at Fortaleza Grande and threw themselves off the cliffs rather than submit to the conquerors. Within a few years the Guanches had effectively been wiped out – though there are those who maintain that they never disappeared and that the present Canario population is largely descended from the Guanches.

Is there such a thing as authentic Canarian cuisine? Away from the standard international choices on offer in the main tourist resorts, a different type of cooking survives in the fishing ports and inland towns and villages of Gran Canaria.

Bananas are not

This is Spanish country cooking, introduced by immigrants and adapted to local ingredients with a few Caribbean influences thrown in – such as the peppers which form an important part of the ubiquitous *mojo* sauce. Herbs and spices are widely used, including garlic, cumin, coriander, saffron, oregano and thyme, while other essential ingredients are olive oil, potatoes and tomatoes.

Bananas, mango, papaya and avocado often appear in salads and desserts and as unusual accompaniments to meat and fish.

Mojo

The standard accompaniment to all Canarian cuisine is *mojo* sauce. This can be bought in jars but most chefs make their own. There are as many

Puerto de Mogán is one of the island's main fishing ports

varieties of *mojo* as there are cooks, with whole recipe books devoted to the subject, but the two basic types are *mojo picón* (spicy red *mojo*) and *mojo verde* (green *mojo*). *Mojo picón* is a blend of chilli peppers, garlic, cumin, paprika and vinegar, served

Paella is a Spanish import which uses seafood and saffron rice

the only fruit...

cold with grilled meat, *gofio*, bread and potatoes. For *mojo verde*, fresh coriander leaves are substituted for the chilli, making it an ideal accompaniment for fish.

Gofio

Gofio, a flour made by grinding toasted barley, maize or wheat, is the traditional Canarian comfort food. This was the staple diet of the Guanches and it has survived almost unchanged to this day. Canarians stir it into warm milk as a breakfast porridge or as a drink for young babies; it is rolled into dumplings and added to soups and stews. It can be kneaded with bananas, blended with wine and egg yolk, or eaten plain with fresh cheese and *mojo* sauce. It can even be made into ice-cream. Although you will not find it on many restaurant menus, *gofio* is the bread-and-butter of Canarian home cooking. Everybody should try it once, but most people seem to agree that once is enough.

Bienmesabe

This popular dessert is made by adding ground almonds and egg yolks to a sugar syrup. Its name means "it tastes good to me". *Bienmesabe* has the consistency

Canarian Specialities

conejo en salmorejo – rabbit marinated in garlic, parsley, oregano, thyme and vinegar, then basted in wine and served in an earthenware dish with ***papas arrugadas***
gofio escaldado – *gofio* stirred into fish stock to produce a thick paste
papas arrugadas – literally "wrinkled" potatoes, boiled in their skins in salty water and eaten with red *mojo* sauce
potaje de berros – watercress soup, which may also include potatoes, sweet potatoes and bacon
puchero canario – a hearty meat and vegetable casserole which typically contains beef, pork, chicken, sausage, chickpeas, marrow, sweetcorn, carrots, beans, tomato, onion and pears, served with *gofio* dumplings to soak up the stock
rancho canario – a stew of meat, potatoes, chickpeas, tomatoes and noodles
ropa vieja – literally "old clothes", this consists of chickpeas fried with diced meat and vegetables and was invented as a way of using up leftovers
sancocho – the most typical Canarian dish of all, this is salt fish and potato stew served with *papas arrugadas*, *gofio* and *mojo* sauce

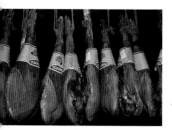

a starter rather than after the meal. The main varieties are *queso tierno* (a soft goat's cheese), *queso curado* (mature sheep's or goat's cheese, such as Majorero from Fuerteventura) and *queso de flor*, produced in the high-lands of Guía and curdled with thistle flowers.

of honey and is often served with baked bananas or poured over ice-cream.

Cheese

In the Canary Islands, *queso* (cheese) is generally eaten as

Fish

Among the Atlantic fish which are caught in the waters off Gran Canaria are *cherne* (a kind of grouper), *sama* (bream) and *vieja* (parrotfish). The most

'it tastes good

common is *cherne*, which is generally casseroled or poached with potatoes and coriander.

In fishing ports such as Arguineguín and Puerto de Mogán, there's always *pescado fresco* (fresh fish) on the menu. This deliberately vague term allows the restaurant to serve whatever the local fishermen have brought in, which will be simply grilled with garlic and herbs and is invariably delicious.

You can buy fresh fish at the Mercado de Vegueta in Las Palmas

o me'

Canarian Recipes
Papas arrugadas
"Wrinkled" potatoes were traditionally cooked in sea-water and it is still the custom to use a large amount of salt to produce a salt crust.

Wash some small potatoes and leave them in their jackets. Add a small amount of water to the pan and a generous sprinkling of coarse sea salt. Bring to the boil, then turn down the heat and simmer slowly until the potatoes are cooked. Drain and gently shake the potatoes until they are dry, wrinkled and coated with salt. Serve with *mojo picón*.

Mojo picón
Seed four fresh red chilli peppers and soak them in hot water for 20 minutes. Pound the chillies together with half a teaspoon of ground cumin, a bulb of peeled garlic and a sprinkling of salt. Add a tablespoon of paprika and continue pounding. Stir well and pour in one cup of olive oil. Stir again and when the mixture becomes a smooth paste, add two cups of wine vinegar and a little water. This recipe can also be made using a food processor and the ingredients can be varied according to taste.

A Snapshot of

The yacht harbour at Las Palmas provides an escape from big city life

Below: Roque Bentaiga at sunset

Right: Guanche caves at Cueva del Rey

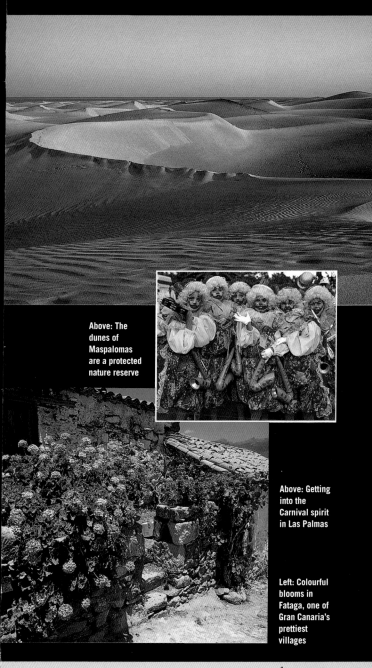

Gran Canaria

Above: The dunes of Maspalomas are a protected nature reserve

Above: Getting into the Carnival spirit in Las Palmas

Left: Colourful blooms in Fataga, one of Gran Canaria's prettiest villages

Although it measures barely 50km across at its widest point, Gran Canaria has often been described as a continent in miniature. Within this small island you find tall mountains, deep valleys, pine and laurel forests, rocky cliffs, sand dunes, barren hillsides and tropical valleys bursting with ripe fruit.

A miniature continent

Above: The Jardín Canario contains many native plant species

The island is almost circular in shape and resembles a volcanic cone, with a summit at the centre and a succession of *barrancos* (gorges) radiating out towards the sea like the spokes of a giant bicycle wheel. The northeasterly trade winds which blow in from the coast bring misty clouds which stack up against the central sierra, dividing the island into the humid north and the parched, sunny south.

Plantlife

With its abundance of microclimates, the island supports a large variety of endemic plants, many of which can be seen at the Jardín Canario near Las Palmas (► 85).

In addition, imported species such as bougainvillea, hibiscus, poinsettia and strelitzia (bird-of-paradise) thrive in the variety of parks and gardens.

The Canary

Travellers are often disappointed to find that the native canary (*serenus canaria*) is actually muddy brown in colour and much quieter than the domesticated songbird, whose yellow plumage and distinctive voice are the result of over 400 years of breeding.

Contrary to popular belief, the canary almost certainly takes its name from the islands rather than the other way round – the Canary Islands probably were named after the large dogs (*canes* in Latin) which the Romans found there when they arrived, or, some say, from the *Canarii*, a Berber tribe.

Bougainvillea makes a wonderful splash of colour

Facing page: Cactus plants grow wild on the rocky hillsides

The island is home to many beautiful varieties of flora

Canarian Flora

There are nearly 2,000 different species of plants in the Canary Islands, of which around 700 are endemic (exclusive to the islands). Many are only of interest to botanists, but the species mentioned below are all quite remarkable and can usually be easily seen.

• **Canary pine** (*pinus canariensis*): this tall pine tree (right) is found in the Central Mountains growing to a height of 60m. Its resinous bark has the ability to survive forest fires, so it can live for hundreds of years. The wood of the Canary pine, known as *tea*, is used in the construction of ceilings and balconies.

• **candelabra spurge** (*euphorbia canariensis*): this cactus-like shrub (inset) is found on rocky hillsides. It has a red fruit and a white milky sap which is used in traditional herbal remedies. It is distinguished by its spindly arms which can grow to heights of 2m.

• **dragon tree** (*dracaena draco*): this distinctive tree (left), with its thick trunk and spiky green crown, is one of the last survivors of the Ice Age. Its blood-red resin was used as a medicine by the Guanches, who named it "dragon's blood" and ascribed it magical powers. There are some fine examples of dragon trees in the Jardín Canario (► 85).

• **white tajinaste** (*echium decaisnei*): a native variety of borage found in dry, rocky areas near the south coast. It has sword-shaped leaves and tiny white flowers which bloom in spring. A related plant, the blue *tajinaste*, grows wild in the Central Mountains.

Lucha Canaria

Two men enter the arena barefoot, each making the sign of the cross as they step onto the sand. They shake hands and grip each other tightly, their right hands clasped together, their left hands clutching the hem of their opponent's rolled-up shorts. An expectant crowd watches. Welcome to *lucha canaria* (Canarian wrestling), the oldest sport in the Canary Islands and one that has been practised since long before the Spanish Conquest.

The sport has its origins in the fights which used to take place between rival Guanche kingdoms and tribes. Chronicles of the conquest describe a wrestling match between fighters from Telde and Gáldar in order to resolve a dispute over grazing rights. It is popular among young people as a symbol of Canarian culture. You can see displays at all the main festivals, and the regular bouts in the local island leagues attract an attendance which is second only to football.

It may look like little more than a brawl, but this is a sport with detailed rules and a strict code of gentlemanly conduct. No part of a wrestler's body other than the soles of his feet may touch the ground and the basic aim is to force your opponent onto the sand. There are 12 players in each team which takes part in a series of best-of-three *bregas* (bouts) to determine the winner. Although strength is important, dexterity and finesse are equally useful. Whatever the outcome, the contest always ends as it began – with a handshake.

Canarian wrestling bouts follow a strict set of rules

Where To See It

You can find out where a Canarian wrestling match is taking place by looking in the local newspapers, especially *La Provincia*, whose Wednesday edition lists all the upcoming weekend fixtures. There are matches most weeks in Las Palmas and all the major towns. For visitors staying in the south coast resorts, the teams to follow are Arguineguín and Maspalomas, who wrestle in the nearby suburb of El Tablero in a *terrero* (sand ring) by the football stadium.

Stick-Fighting

Juego del palo (stick-fighting) is another traditional Canarian sport with its origins in the ancient art of duelling. Two men face one another with *garrotes* (2m-long wooden staffs). The idea is to strike your opponent with the stick while at the same time dodging the blows. Although it is no longer practised as a sport, you can sometimes see demonstrations at local fiestas in Gran Canaria.

If you have ever wondered why people go fishing, take a stroll around the harbour at Puerto Rico as the sport-fishing boats come in and watch the emotion etched into the faces. There is disappointment from those who have returned empty-handed; elation from those who have made a catch; and every now and then, a surge of quiet pride and satisfaction from an amateur fisherman who has just landed the catch of his life.

Dreaming of

Puerto Rico is one of the world capitals of big game fishing. More than 30 world records have been set here. Billboards on the quayside detail the latest catches. Among the fish which swim in the waters off the south coast of Gran Canaria are albacora, big-eye, yellowfin and skipjack tuna, bonito, barracuda, swordfish, shark and wahoo, but the ultimate prize is the blue marlin, which can weigh anything between 250 and 500kg. To see a blue marlin being caught is to witness an epic sporting battle between man and beast which you are never quite sure who is going to win.

How To Get The Big Catch

The best time to hunt for marlin is between May and October, while tuna are mostly caught during the winter. Several boats offer daily fishing trips throughout the year from the two harbours at Puerto Rico. Most trips depart at 9 am and last for around six hours, though some operators offer sunset

Local fishing has been part of life in Las Palmas for decades (left) and the popular sport-fishing at Puerto Rico (above)

the big catch

trips leaving at 3 pm. As a rule it is best to book three or four days ahead. Prices vary but so do your chances of success, so it is worth shopping around.

Rods, tackle and bait are provided, and most boats are equipped with an outrigger, fighting chairs and sonic navigational equipment. You just need to take food, water and warm clothing. Be aware that anything you catch belongs to the skipper. Most captains operate a strict tag-and-release policy as far as blue marlin is concerned.

If you don't want to fish, most boats will also accept paying spectators at a slightly lower price. Apart from the excitement of watching the fishermen at work, there is a good chance of spotting basking dolphins and possibly flying fish.

Sport-Fishing Boats
Barrakuda Dos (tel: 928 735080)
Blue Marlin III (tel: 928 560627)
Dorado (tel: 928 565521)
Katfish (tel: 607 266941)

Music, colour, fancy dress... it's Carnival time in Las Palmas

Fies

Carnival

Nowhere in Spain is the traditional pre-Lenten Carnival celebrated with as much gusto as it is in the Canary Islands. Banned under the Franco dictatorship, Carnival is back with a vengeance. Each year Gran Canaria and Tenerife compete to stage the biggest parades this side of Rio de Janerio.

For nearly three weeks in February, Las Palmas is one giant party, with acrobats, clowns, magicians, brass bands, salsa music, fireworks and riotous fancy-dress parades.

The dates vary from year to year, but it all starts around nine weeks before Easter with the Verbena de la Sábana (Sheet Party), where participants are dressed in a sheet and little else. Like most of the Carnival events, this takes place on an open-air stage in Parque Santa Catalina (► 69). It is followed by the election of the Carnival Queen and the Children's Queen and a week of street parties, singing contests and body-painting competitions leading up to the final weekend.

The wildest night of all is the Friday before Shrove Tuesday, when the Carnival Drag Queen is chosen. The grand parade takes place the following day, with the

Children often take part in the Carnival parades

Carne Vale
The word "Carnival" derives
from the Italian *carne vale*,
meaning "farewell to meat" – the idea
being that this is a final excuse for feasting
and frivolous behaviour before the fasting
and self-denial of Lent.

Carnival Queen on the leading float in a glittering outfit
of sequins, spangles and
feathers. The parade starts in
La Isleta and continues for
several hours, ending at
midnight with an open-air
mogollón (fancy-dress
party). Most of Las
Palmas joins in,
wearing outrageous
masks and costumes.

Sunday is the
day of the children's
Carnival, while
Monday sees the
start of the Velatorio
(death watch), when a
huge papier-mâché sar-
dine is carried in mock
funeral procession
through the streets
by a group of
mourners dressed in
black drag. The Burial
of the Sardine, which
symbolises the end of
Carnival and the
beginning of Lent, takes place
on Shrove Tuesday on Playa
de las Canteras (➤ 70), to the

**Rio de Janeiro comes to Las
Palmas for a few weeks each year**

Some people spend all year working on their costumes

accompaniment of bonfires and fireworks.

Carnival may have ended in Las Palmas but it continues further south, with a weekend of processions and parties around the Yumbo Centre in Playa del Inglés (➤ 148).

The Virgin of the Cave

The last Sunday in August witnesses the climax of the fiesta of the Virgin of the Cave in Artenara. At the beginning of the fiesta, the carved wooden statue of the Virgin is taken out of her cave chapel and placed in the parish church, where the villagers come all week to pay their respects. The priest gives his blessing, the worshippers file out and the Virgin is carried around the town by four hefty men, accompanied by a brass

"There are no men in Las Palmas in February. Everyone is either a woman, or dressed as one."

Canario musician in conversation

band, a military guard of honour, an occasional burst of fireworks and a procession of civic dignitaries in suits.

A folklore performance entertains the crowds and is broadcast live on Canary Islands television. Folk groups from Gran Canaria and Tenerife sing and dance *isas* and *malagueñas*, dressed in extravagantly embroidered waistcoats and skirts. As dusk falls, people climb to the *mirador* above the village to watch the sun set over Tenerife.

At 9 pm the concert ends and the final procession begins. A burst of fireworks lights up the night sky and dozens of flaming torches spring into life as the mayor lights the touch-paper. The Virgin is carried slowly back to her cave, with more music and fireworks followed by a solemn, torchlit climb. Every few metres the priest pauses to say the *Ave Maria* ten times.

Below: Inside the chapel at Artenara

La Rama

One of the chroniclers of the conquest recalled how the Guanche priests "gathered the people together and led them to the sea-shore, with boughs and branches in their hands, calling out loud as they beat the water with their boughs." This tradition is still carried out today at the fiestas of La Rama in Agaete (▶ 102) and San Nicolás de Tolentino (▶ 144).

As the procession reaches the chapel, the fireworks go off once again, a spectacular display which lasts for 20 minutes. The Virgin is placed back in her chapel, the priest says his final blessings and the villagers return to the square to salsa the night away.

The cave chapel at Artenara is the setting for a spectacular fiesta

Ten Special Experiences

• Walking barefoot across the Dunas de Maspalomas (➤ 132) with the sun in your face and the wind in your hair
• Looking out for those friendly dolphins on a game-fishing trip from Puerto Rico (➤ 142)
• The drive up the Barranco de Fataga (➤ 140), followed by the circuit through the

• Folk singing and dancing at the Pueblo Canario in Las Palmas (➤ 68)
• Watching the sun set over the west coast, with Tenerife rising romantically out of the sea

Five Great Places To Watch The Sunset...

• Cruz de Tejeda, from the hill behind El Refugio Hotel (➤ 43)

The best of...

mountains from Ayacata to Cruz de Tejeda (➤ 115)
• Climbing Roque Nublo (➤ 112) to see the whole island spread out beneath you
• The first sight you get of Puerto de Mogán (➤ 138) from the sea
• Eating fresh fish by the harbourside in one of the island's fishing ports
• Tasting a plate of *papas arrugadas* with *mojo* sauce
• The passion and excitement of a traditional Canarian fiesta (➤ 28)

• Tamadaba pine forest (➤ 108)
• The lighthouse at Maspalomas (➤ 132)
• The harbour at Puerto de la Aldea (➤ 144)
• The cliff path from Puerto Rico to Playa de los Amadores (➤ 143)

...And Five More Great Views

• Artenara (➤ 108) – the view of the central sierra from the Rio de Janeiro-style statue of Christ

Left: A walk across the Maspalomas sand dunes

Centre: The view from Artenara takes in Roque Nublo and Roque Bentaiga

• Mirador del Balcón (➤ 93) – the view over the wild west coast
• Pico de Bandama – the view over the crater from its height of 574m
• Playa del Inglés (➤ 129) – the view across the dunes from the mirador behind the Riu Palace Maspalomas Hotel (➤ 44)
• Puerto de las Nieves (➤ 93) – the view over the harbour from the road to San Nicolás de Tolentino

Gran Canaria On Disc
• Los Gofiones, *30 Años* (Manzana, 1998): 30 years of the best in traditional Canarian folk music by six generations of musicians

• Mestisay, *Viento de la Isla* (EMI, 1998): Cool Latin jazz and female vocals by a group better known for their performances of Canarian folk songs

The Five Best Nightspots...
• Casino Las Palmas, Hotel Santa Catalina, Las Palmas (➤ 41)
• Pacha, Calle Simón Bolívar, Las Palmas
• Joy, Metro Centre, Playa del Inglés (➤ 148)
• Pacha, Metro Centre, Playa del Inglés (➤ 148)
• Yumbo Centre, Playa del Inglés (➤ 148)

The Five Best Restaurants...
• Casa Montesdeoca, Las Palmas (➤ 71)
• Casa Pepe El Breca II, Playa del Inglés (➤ 145)
• El Alpendre, Santa Lucía
• El Padrino, Las Palmas (➤ 71)
• La Bodeguilla Juananá, Puerto de Mogán (➤ 146)

Top: The ascent of Roque Nublo is a popular weekend walk

Above: The best way to arrive in Puerto Mogán is by boat

- that the first known reference to Gran Canaria is found in an account by the Roman historian **Pliny the Elder** (AD 23–79)? He described the Canarian archipelago as "the Fortunate Isles" and named the main island Canaria, possibly because of the dogs (*canes* in Latin) which were found living there and which are still portrayed on the coat of arms of the Canary Islands.

- that the Canary Islands are less than 200km from Morocco but more than 1,500km from the Spanish capital Madrid – which itself is closer to London than Las Palmas?

- that Gran Canaria is the only place in Europe where you'll find **date palms** from north Africa as well as **cactus plants** from Mexico growing

Did you know...?

- that on **maps** from the 2nd century AD until the discovery of America in 1492, the Canary Islands were marked as the westernmost point of the known world?

- that there are references to Canary **wine** in the plays of Shakespeare and the poetry of John Keats?

- that in a study by Thomas Whitmore of the University of Syracuse (USA) in 1996, Las Palmas was named as the city with the most pleasing **climate** in the world?

- that the first **moon landing** by Neil Armstrong in 1969 was tracked by NASA scientists from the space centre at Pasito Blanco?

- that as well as meaning a canary and an inbabitant of the Canary Islands, *canario* is an archaic Spanish phrase meaning "Well, I'll be blowed"?

- that each square metre of **beach** is worth over £80,000 in tourist turnover?

wild in the mountains and valleys?

- that a BBC programme claimed in 2000 that an eruption within the next few thousand years will make La Palma crash into the sea, causing a *tsunami* (tidal wave) that may destroy the US coast from Miami to New York?

The clear skies above Gran Canaria are tracked from the NASA space station at Pasito Blanco

Poetic Justice
*Have ye tippled drink more fine
Than mine host's Canary wine?*
John Keats
Lines on the Mermaid Tavern
(1820)

First Two Hours

Arriving at Gando Airport

The main point of entry is the **Aeropuerto de Gando**, 22km south of Las Palmas on the east coast of the island.

- Most travellers on package holidays are met at the airport by representatives of the **tour operator** and transported to their accommodation by bus.
- The major **car hire** companies have desks in the arrivals hall, and there are also currency exchange facilities.

Getting to Las Palmas from Gando Airport

- The quickest but most expensive option is to take a **taxi** from outside the airport building.
- There is also a frequent, reliable and inexpensive **bus** service to Las Palmas. Bus No 60 leaves from outside the airport terminal every 30 minutes from 6.30 am–9 pm and then hourly until 2 am. The journey takes around 30 minutes. The buses arrive at the central bus station beside Parque San Telmo, where there are connections to local buses and taxis as well as buses to the rest of the island.

Getting to the South Coast from Gando Airport

- The quickest but most expensive option is to take a **taxi** from outside the airport building. Costs vary.
- The other alternative is to get there by **bus**. Bus No 66 leaves for Playa del Inglés every two hours from 7.15 am–9.15 pm. The journey takes around one hour. From Playa del Inglés there are regular connections to other south coast resorts, including Puerto Rico and Puerto de Mogán.

Car Hire

- The major car hire companies have offices at the **airport**.
- You will generally save both time and money by **booking in advance**.
- To hire a car you must be **over 21**, and you will need a credit card, passport and driving licence.
- Car hire is **widely available** in Las Palmas and all the main resorts, so unless you are staying somewhere remote, it may be better to travel to your accommodation by bus and hire a car when you get there.
- **4WD** cars are available in all the main resorts but you need to book them in advance at the airport.
- If you are driving from the airport, the **GC1 motorway** leads north to Las Palmas and south to Playa del Inglés.

Avis: tel: 928 579578; www.avis.com
Europcar: tel: 922 372882; www.europcar.com
Hertz: tel: 928 579577; www.hertz.com

Arriving by Sea

- **Passenger and car ferries** from the Spanish mainland and the other Canary Islands arrive at Puerto de la Luz in Las Palmas.
- There is also a **fast ferry link** from Tenerife to Puerto de las Nieves, with a free shuttle bus to Las Palmas. The journey from Puerto de las Nieves to Las Palmas takes around 40 minutes by car.

Security

Although Gran Canaria is no more dangerous than other popular tourist areas of Spain, it is important to remember that you are at your most vulnerable to theft when you first arrive in an unfamiliar destination.

- It is advisable to keep your passport, money and other valuables in an inside pocket or money-belt and to lock them in a **safety deposit box** as soon as you arrive at your hotel or apartment.
- Keep your **hand luggage**, including items such as cameras, with you at all times.
- Do not leave any bags **unattended** while standing at a car hire desk or loading suitcases onto a bus.
- **Petty crime** is particularly prevalent in the Santa Catalina and port districts of Las Palmas.

Tourist Information Offices

Most tourist office staff speak excellent English, and can issue maps and information in English.

Las Palmas

- The **main tourist office** is situated in Parque Santa Catalina, in an old-style Canarian building beside the terminus for the Guagua Turística tour buses. Open: Mon–Fri 9–2, tel: 928 264623.
- The **Patronato de Turismo** (Tourist Board) has its offices at Calle León y Castillo 17, a short walk from the bus station. Open: Mon–Fri 9–2, tel: 928 219600.
- There are also **tourist information offices** and kiosks in Parque San Telmo, Plaza de Santa Ana and Avenida Mesa y López as well as at the Pueblo Canario and on the promenade behind Playa las Canteras.
- The information office at the **bus station** has maps and timetables, and sells discount tickets such as the *Bono-Guagua* and *Tarjeta Insular* (➤ 38).

South Coast

- **Yumbo Centre**, Playa del Inglés, tel: 928 771550. Open: Mon–Fri 9–9, Sat 9–2.
- **Mirador Campo de Golf**, Maspalomas, tel: 928 769585. Open: Mon–Fri 9–9, Sat 9–2.
- **Puerto Rico**, near the bus stop on the roundabout at the entrance to the resort, tel: 928 560029. Open: Mon–Fri 9–7, Sat 10–1.

Getting Around

The island's comparatively small size can be an advantage. Both Las Palmas and Maspalomas are just 30 minutes from the airport, and it is quite possible to drive round the whole island in a day (➤ 164).

Buses

For journeys to and from Las Palmas and the south coast resorts, the most economic and efficient way of getting about is by bus.

- The bus company, **Global**, operates a comprehensive network of routes, with regular departures during the day and some night services.
- **Timetables and maps** are available from the bus station in Las Palmas and the tourist office in Playa del Inglés.

■ The *Tarjeta Insular* discount card is good value for anyone travelling around the island by bus. The *Tarjeta Insular* is available from the bus station in Las Palmas and at kiosks and shops where the Tarjeta Insular symbol is displayed. It gives around 12 Euros' worth of travel at a 30 per cent discount. To use the card, simply tell the driver where you are going and insert the card into the machine at the front of the bus so that the fare can be deducted from your remaining credit.

Some of the most **useful bus lines** are:
01 Las Palmas–Playa del Inglés–Puerto Rico–Puerto de Mogán
30 Las Palmas–Playa del Inglés–Maspalomas
32 Playa del Inglés–Puerto Rico–Puerto de Mogán
61 Las Palmas–Playa del Inglés–Puerto Rico–Puerto de Mogán (night bus)

City Buses

Las Palmas has its own bus company, **Guaguas Municipales**, which operates a network of routes throughout the city.
■ Fares are flat-rate, but the ***Bono-Guagua*** discount card, available from newsagents, tobacconists and bus terminals, gives ten journeys for the price of six. The *Tarjeta Insular* (see above) is also valid on city buses.
■ The three **main routes** connect the old town to the port district. The most useful is No 1, which operates 24 hours a day and follows a direct route from Teatro Pérez Galdós to Parque San Telmo, Pueblo Canario and Parque Santa Catalina. Bus Nos. 2 and 3 depart from Alameda de Colón and also pass through Parque Santa Catalina.
■ A detailed **city bus map** and **timetable** is available from the information office at the bus station beside Parque San Telmo.
■ The ***Guagua Turística*** is an open-top tour bus which makes a two-hour circuit of the city, beginning and ending in Parque Santa Catalina. Tickets are valid for a day and you can hop on and off as often as you like. The bus leaves Parque Santa Catalina every 30 minutes from 9.30–12.30 and 2.45–5.45. You can also pick up the bus outside the central bus station on Parque San Telmo.

Taxis

■ Taxis can be identified by a **green light** on the top which when illuminated indicates thatthey are available for hire.
■ For local journeys, fares are **metered** and charges are usually reasonable.
■ If travelling outside municipal boundaries, the meter does not apply and it is best to **fix a fare in advance**.
■ You can usually **hail a taxi** on the street, but at busy times it is better to find a taxi rank or to book in advance.

Useful telephone numbers include:
■ 928 462212 (Las Palmas)
■ 928 766767 (Maspalomas/Playa del Inglés)
■ 928 152740 (Puerto Rico)
■ 928 735000 (Puerto de Mogán)

Driving

If you want to explore the interior of Gran Canaria away from the coastal resorts, you will probably need to hire a car (► 36).

- Driving in the **mountains** can be a challenge, with twisting roads and narrow bends demanding intense concentration.
- Make sure you allow **plenty of time** for your journey and do not expect to cover more than 40km per hour.
- The only **fast roads** on the island are the GC1 motorway from Las Palmas to Arguineguín and the GC2 from Las Palmas to Agaete.

Car Hire

- The **major international** car hire companies have offices at Gando Airport (➤ 36), in Las Palmas and in all the main resorts.
- **Local companies** also offer competitive deals, so unless you need a car immediately it is worth shopping around when you reach your resort.
- To **hire a car** you will need your passport, driving licence and credit card. Keep these papers on you at all times, along with the car hire documents.
- Check your **insurance cover** carefully. If you plan to drive on mountain tracks or to some of the more remoter beaches, you will not be covered unless you hire a jeep or off-road (4WD) vehicle.

Driving Essentials

- Drive on the **right-hand** side of the road.
- **Seat belts** are compulsory for the driver and all passengers.
- The legal **alcohol** limit is 80mg alcohol per 100ml blood.
- **Speed limits** are 120kph on motorways, 90kph on main roads and 40kph in urban areas, unless otherwise indicated.
- **Dipped headlights** are compulsory in tunnels.
- Use your **horn** when overtaking and when approaching blind bends.
- **Petrol** is much cheaper than on mainland Spain. Many petrol stations are open 24 hours. There are few in the mountains, so fill up before you head inland. Most stations accept credit cards.
- **Parking** is prohibited on white or yellow lines. Blue lines indicate a restricted parking area where you must purchase a ticket from a pay-and-display machine.
- **Theft** from hire cars is widespread. Never leave any items on display inside the car, and lock all valuables out of sight in the boot.

Organised Excursions

- Package tour operators offer numerous **excursions**, from jeep safaris to coach tours, which can be booked through your holiday representative.
- The **advantage** is that you can get around the island without hiring a car; the **drawbacks** are that they are expensive and you have no control over the itinerary.
- **Beware** of local companies offering free excursions – these are invariably combined with a hard-sell timeshare (➤ 40) or product demonstration.

Admission Charges

The unit of currency is the Euro, introduced as legal tender in January 2002. The *peseta* will cease to be legal tender in June 2002 (➤ 171). The exchange rate is 100 pesetas = 0.60 Euros. The cost of admission for museums and places of interest featured in the guide is indicated by the following price categories.

Inexpensive = under 3 Euros
Moderate = 3–6 Euros
Expensive = over 6 Euros

Accommodation

Most people arrive in Gran Canaria on package holidays with pre-booked accommodation. The majority of hotels and apartments are booked up by tour operators, so independent travellers may experience difficulties in finding somewhere to stay.

Local tourist offices keep lists of apartments and may be able to help, but on the whole it is far better to book in advance.

Hotels

All hotels are officially graded by the Canarian government from one to five stars, with most establishments rated as three-star or higher. In three-star hotels and above, all rooms will have a private bathroom.

The hotels on the following pages have been selected because of their quality or special character. Hotels are more expensive during the peak season from November to April. There is a second peak in July and August, when many Spanish families are on holiday. The quietest months are May, June, September and October.

Apartments

Many people, especially families, prefer the freedom of a self-catering apartment or villa. Apartments are graded from one to three keys, and even the simplest will usually have a bedroom, bathroom, lounge, kitchenette and balcony. Bed linen, towels and maid service are included in the price; equipment such as kettles and toasters can sometimes be hired for an extra charge. Aparthotels are large apartment blocks with all the facilities of a hotel, such as a swimming pool, restaurant and evening entertainment.

The majority of self-catering accommodation is pre-booked by package tourists, but if you ask around in a resort you may be able to find apartments to let.

Casas rurales

Casas rurales are village houses, cave dwellings and farmsteads which have been converted into holiday cottages for rent. If you don't mind hiring a car and being based away from the beach, these are good value and offer a more authentic experience of Gran Canaria. Most are decorated in traditional style, though many also have swimming pools. Rural houses can be let through the following agencies:

Gran Canaria Rural (tel: 928 460889)
Grantural (tel: 928 494411)
Retur (tel: 928 661668)

Timeshare

Persistent salespeople in the main resorts will invite you to demonstrations of timeshare properties, sometimes described as "vacation ownership". This involves buying the right to an annual holiday in a particular villa or apartment in return for a one-off down payment and an annual service charge. Some of the timeshare properties, such as those at Anfi del Mar, are extremely well designed and maintained, but you should be aware that the combined cost of service charge, flights, insurance and loss of interest can make this an expensive way of paying for your holiday. You should also think carefully about whether you want to spend your holiday in the same place every year.

> **Prices**
> The symbols refer to the average cost of a double room in high season, generally November to April. All prices exclude 4.5 per cent sales tax (IGIC).
>
> £ under 60 Euros ££ 60–120 Euros £££ over 120 Euros

List of Places to Stay

Las Palmas

Madrid £

For those who put character before comfort, this rambling old colonial hotel on one of Las Palmas' most attractive squares is the only place to stay. The antique furniture and old-style wooden beds have probably been in place since 1936, when General Franco spent his last night here before launching the Spanish Civil War. Ask for a room with a balcony overlooking the square – though it can get noisy at night.

➕ 183 E2 ✉ Plaza de Cairasco 4
☎ 928 360664; fax: 928 382176

Parque ££

This hotel facing Parque San Telmo is convenient for the old town and makes a good base for excursions around the island as the bus station is just one minute away. The rooms are comfortable and modern and some of them have views over the park. There are more good views from the top-floor restaurant and the rooftop sun terrace. This is the best choice in Las Palmas in the medium-price bracket.

➕ 183 E3 ✉ Muelle de Las Palmas 2
☎ 928 368000; fax: 928 368856

Reina Isabel £££

The best of the hotels on Las Canteras beach has been thoroughly modernised and is once again a stylish place to stay. The rooftop pool is ideal for soaking up the sun and the hotel also has private sunbeds and parasols on the beach. The top-floor restaurant features inventive modern Spanish cuisine, and a beachside terrace café has sandwiches and snacks. Most of the rooms have balconies overlooking the sea.

➕ 182 B4 ✉ Calle Alfredo L Jones 40
☎ 928 260100; fax: 928 274558

Santa Catalina £££

Royalty and heads of state have traditionally been attracted to this old-world hotel, which first opened in 1890. Dark wooden balconies look down over tropical gardens, and the wicker chairs on the veranda are a good place to take cocktails or after-noon tea. Facilities include a pool, sauna, casino and a daily courtesy bus to the beach, 2km away. Parque Doramas, which is spread out behind the hotel, makes a peaceful place for a stroll.

➕ 183 D5 ✉ Calle León y Castillo 227
☎ 928 243040; fax: 928 242764; e-mail:
hsantacatalina@entorno.es

The North

Arucas

La Hacienda del Buen Suceso ££

This smart, rural hotel, opened in 1999, is set in a manor house at the centre of one of Gran Canaria's largest banana plantations. There are only 18 rooms so it never feels crowded and there is always plenty of space around the pool. Horse-riding and mountain bikes are available, and guests are also allowed to wander around the estate. This is where people come to be pampered away from the crowds.

➕ 179 D5 ✉ Carretera de Arucas a
Bañaderos, km1 ☎ 928 622945; fax:
928 692942;
e-mail: hacienda@idecnet.com

Caldera de Bandama

Bandama Golf & Country Hotel ££

The small hotel beside Las Palmas golf club overlooks the crater of Bandama on one side and the golf course on the other. The first tee is just a few metres from the hotel entrance. Not surprisingly, most people come here to play golf, but other options include tennis, horse-riding and swimming in the heated pool. For golfers, green fees can be included in the daily rate. Golf competitions for guests are held every week.

➕ 179 E4 ✉ Caldera de Bandama
☎ 928 353354; fax: 928 351290;
e-mail: bandama@golfhotell.com

Puerto de las Nieves

Puerto de las Nieves ££

This luxury hotel and hydrotherapy centre opened in 2000. Guests have free access to the spa pool and sauna, while optional extras include massage, reflexology and facials and various specialist anti-stress treatments. Most of the 30 rooms have a sea-facing terrace, and the beach is just a couple of minutes away. The restaurant features Spanish and Canarian cuisine based on local produce from the Valle de Agaete.

➕ 178 B5 ✉ Avenida Alcalde José de Armas ☎ 928 886256; fax: 928 886267; e-mail: hpnieves@idecnet.com

Valle de Agaete

Princesa Guayarmina £

The spa hotel at the head of the valley offers a range of treatments including acupuncture, hydromassage and Turkish baths. The restaurant features traditional Canarian cooking as well as vegetarian meals using fresh produce from the hotel farm. This is a real get-away-from-it-all destination for a healthy holiday, with walks in the mountains and wonderful views out to sea. There is also a small outdoor pool. The shop sells an interesting selection of Canarian books and CDs.

➕ 178 C4 ✉ Los Berrazales ☎ 928 898009; fax: 928 898525

Centre and South

Agüimes

Casa de los Camellos £

A 300-year-old stone barn in the heart of Agüimes has been turned into a delightful rural hotel, whose 12 rooms with traditional wooden balconies are set around interior courtyards and gardens. Agüimes has become something of a centre for rural tourism in Gran Canaria, and several houses have been converted into *casas rurales* (➤ 40).

➕ 179 E3 ✉ Calle Progreso 12
☎ 928 785003; fax: 928 785053;
e-mail: hrcamellos@hecansa.org

Arguineguín

La Canaria £££

One of the top hotels on the island is owned by the Steigenberger chain and this is reflected in the largely German clientele. All of the rooms have balconies looking out to sea across luxuriant gardens with interconnecting pools. Children are well catered for with a children's pool and a play area with table tennis and table football. The hotel has its own small cove beach but the bigger beach at Patalavaca is just a short walk away.

➕ 178 C1 ✉ Barranco de la Verga
☎ 928 150400; fax: 928 151003;
e-mail: reservas@lacanaria.com

Barranco de Fataga

Molino del Agua de Fataga £

This rural hotel is situated in a magnificent palm grove, in a group of converted farm buildings overlooking the restored *gofio* mill from which it takes its name. The rooms are decorated in traditional style, with iron furniture made by a blacksmith who works on the premises. Rooms are small, simple and pretty, with their own wooden balcony or terrace. Camel rides are available, and a children's playground has goats, peacocks and hens. The restaurant serves Canarian mountain cuisine on a poolside terrace.

🔶 179 D2 ✉ Carretera de Fataga a San Bartolomé, km1 ☎ 928 172089; fax: 928 172244

Cruz de Tejeda

El Refugio £

If you are planning a walking holiday in the mountains, this alpine lodge is by far the best place to stay. There are only ten rooms, decorated in Canarian style but with all modern comforts. There is a small pool in the garden, and a cosy lounge with books, games, and coffee-making facilities. Climb the path behind the hotel at night for sunset views of Tenerife. This is a very peaceful place at night.

🔶 178 C4 ✉ Cruz de Tejeda ☎ 928 666513; fax: 928 666520

Maspalomas

Grand Hotel Residencia £££

Opened in 2000, this small designer hotel has quickly become established as one of the most exclusive addresses on the island. The rooms are set around the pool inside Spanish-Moorish villas with wooden balconies and colonial-style furnishings. A wellness centre offers mud baths, thalassotherapy and Chinese medicine, and the restaurant has a five-course menu of modern Mediterranean cuisine. Added touches include internet access and CD players in the rooms, and copies of artist Joan Miró's works on the walls.

🔶 179 D1 ✉ Avenida del Oasis 32 ☎ 928 723100; fax: 928 723108; e-mail: residencia@a1web.es

Maspalomas Oasis £££

Long considered the top hotel on the south coast, the Maspalomas Oasis has 65,000sq m of gardens in the heart of the Oasis palm grove.

Sunloungers are scattered throughout the grounds, where peacocks strut and guests practise their ping-pong and putting. This has all the facilities you would expect of a five-star hotel, including 24-hour room service, evening entertainment and satellite TV, as well as a billiards room, children's club and special touches, such as occasional summer barbecues by the lake.

🔶 179 D1 ✉ Playa de Maspalomas ☎ 928 141448; fax: 928 141192

Riu Palace Meloneras £££

This huge complex of 300 hotel rooms and 144 villas was the first to open in the new resort of Las Meloneras. The tone is set by the extravagant lobby, all cut-glass chandeliers and polished stone. The extensive gardens feature two swimming pools, a play area and access to the seafront promenade. The beach at Maspalomas is a short walk away. Guests staying in the villas have access to all the hotel facilities, which include tennis, table tennis and bike hire.

🔶 178 C1 ✉ Urbanización Las Meloneras ☎ 928 143182; fax: 928 142544

Palmitos Parque

Helga Masthoff Park & Sport Hotel £££

The former German tennis champion Helga Masthoff has established a sports hotel among the subtropical gardens above Palmitos Parque. As well as six artificial grass tennis courts, there is a golf school with putting green, bunker and pitching area in the gardens. The health club features saunas, massage and jacuzzis as well as a naturist zone. There are good walks in the nearby mountains, and bicycles can be hired for excursions. All of the rooms have balconies overlooking the valley.

🔶 178 C2 ✉ Barranco de los Palmitos ☎ 928 142100; fax: 928 141114; e-mail: h-masthoff-hotel@ctv.es

Playa del Inglés

Riu Palace Maspalomas £££

Standing on the edge of the Maspalomas sand dunes, this imposing white hotel has all the appearance of a Moorish palace. It has 342 rooms and a full range of facilities, including sauna, beauty salon and an elegant shopping arcade. A short walk over the dunes leads to the beach, a longer trek to the lighthouse at Maspalomas. Many of the rooms have sea views offering great sunset vistas of the dunes.

➕ 179 D1 ✉ Avenida de Tirajana ☎ 928 769500; fax: 928 769800

Puerto de Mogán

Club de Mar ££

This small hotel on the quayside has 56 double rooms as well as apartments in the villas behind the port. All of the apartments have a rooftop sun terrace and access to hotel facilities including the pool. From the pool area you can dive straight into the sea off Puerto de Mogán's small beach. If the hotel is full, ask around at the waterfront bars and cafés, several of which have villas and apartments for rent.

➕ 178 B2 ✉ Playa de Mogán ☎ 928 565066; fax: 928 565438

San Agustín

Gloria Palace ££

This hotel has the largest thalassotherapy centre in Europe, with five sea-water pools and treatments ranging from seaweed therapy to Chinese acupuncture and ultrasonic marine baths. There is a long walk to the beach, about 15 minutes away across a main road, though there is a courtesy bus available. A panoramic restaurant specialises in Basque and French cuisine.

➕ 179 D1 ✉ Las Margaritas ☎ 928 768300; fax: 928 767929; e-mail: gloriapalace@hvsl.es

San Bartolomé de Tirajana

Las Tirajanas ££

Set in a commanding position at the head of the Barranco de Tirajana, this modern hotel is a good example of the shift towards rural tourism. Up in the mountains you are completely away from it all, yet in less than an hour you can be on the beach. Most rooms have balconies overlooking the gorge, with views down to the coast. The sun terrace has a small heated pool.

➕ 179 D3 ✉ San Bartolomé de Tirajana ☎ 928 127401; fax: 928 123023; e-mail: lastirajanas@eresmas.com

Food and Drink

Most restaurants in Gran Canaria offer Canarian cuisine (► 16), together with steaks, seafood dishes and traditional Spanish favourites such as *paella*. Fresh fish is available all around the coast, particularly in fishing ports such as Puerto de las Nieves, Puerto de Mogán and Arguineguín.

What and Where to Eat

- In the mountainous interior, the most common type of restaurant is a *parrilla*, a country-style grill specialising in barbecued, grilled and roasted meat.
- Resorts such as Puerto Rico and Playa del Inglés have a **full range of restaurants**, offering English breakfasts, hamburgers, pizzas, apple strudel and other reminders of home to an international clientele.
- Bars in Las Palmas and other towns serve *tapas*, small portions of Spanish and Canarian snacks which can often take the place of a meal.

These originated in the old Spanish custom of placing a free *tapa* (lid) of food, such as a saucer of olives, over a drink. Popular *tapas* include *pata de cerdo* (cold roast pork) and *queso curado* (mature cheese).

- One snack which is available everywhere, even in tourist areas, is **papas arrugadas** (salty boiled potatoes with *mojo* sauce – ➤ 19).
- The best places to buy **picnic food** are at the Mercado de Vegueta in Las Palmas (➤ 66), the weekly market at Vega de San Mateo (➤ 96), and supermarkets in all the main resorts.

Eating Out – A Practical Guide

- The traditional **mealtimes** are 1–4 pm for lunch and 8–11 pm for dinner, though many restaurants are open throughout the day to cater for the varying demands of locals and tourists.
- Many restaurants offer a **menu del día**, a fixed-price menu of three courses with water or wine included. This is always available at lunchtime and sometimes in the evening, and usually represents good value.
- By law, **service** has to be included in the price, though there may be a nominal cover charge for items such as bread and olives. If you are happy with the service, it is customary to leave a tip of between 5 and 10 per cent. In bars, the tradition is to leave some small change on the counter.
- **Booking** is rarely necessary except at the smartest restaurants, though it is usually worth booking a table for Saturday dinner or Sunday lunch.
- **Vegetarians** could have a hard time as even vegetable dishes often contain pieces of meat or fish. Most restaurants are happy to serve you a large *ensalada mixta* (mixed salad) with *tortilla* (potato omelette) or *queso* (cheese).
- It is **quite acceptable** to order two starters and no main course, or a single starter for two people to share.
- **Children's menus** are available in some of the resort restaurants, but if not you can always ask for a smaller portion of an adult dish.

A Guide to Drinking

- **Mineral water** is produced in Firgas and Teror and is available across the island. Ask for *agua sin gas* (still) or *agua con gas* (sparkling).
- The variety of fruit grown on Gran Canaria means that fresh **fruit juice** is always a good choice. The most common is *zumo de naranja* (orange juice), though some bars offer freshly squeezed mango, papaya, banana, pineapple and kiwi fruit.
- **Coffee** is usually served after the meal as *café solo*, a small shot of strong, black coffee like an espresso. Other varieties are *café cortado* (espresso with a dash of hot milk), *café con leche* (with lots of hot milk) and *café con leche condensada* (with condensed milk).
- The most popular brand of **beer** is Tropical, which is produced in Gran Canaria and comes either in bottles or on draught. Most bars also stock a range of imported beers.
- Small quantities of **wine** are produced on Gran Canaria and the other Canary Islands. One unusual choice is *malvasia* (malmsey), a white wine from Lanzarote which can be sweet or dry. The best wines from the Spanish mainland come from the region of La Rioja.
- The local **spirit** is rum from Arucas, the base for a number of liqueurs, including *ron miel* (honey rum) and *guindilla* (cherry liqueur). Spanish brandy is also popular and is sometimes added to *sangría*, a red wine and fruit punch.
- It is the custom in many restaurants to bring you a small glass of **liqueur** with your bill.

Best...

...for fish:
Casa Pepe El Breca II, Lomo Maspalomas, Carretera de Fataga (► 145);
El Padrino, Calle Jesús Nazareno 1, Las Colorades (► 71);
La Cofradía de Pescadores, Puerto de Mogán (► 146)
...for meat:
El Secuestro, Avenida Cabildo Insular 26, Teror (► 100);
Las Cumbres, Avenida de Tirajana, Playa del Inglés (► 145);
Yolanda, Cruz de Tejeda (► 119)
...for views:
La Silla, Carretera La Silla 9, Artenara (► 119);
Las Nasas, Calle Nuestra Señora de las Nieves 6, Puerto de las Nieves
(► 100);
Tagoror, Montaña de las Tierras, Barranco de Guayadeque (► 145)
...for tapas:
El Herreño, Calle Mendizábal 5, Las Palmas (► 71)
...for vegetarians:
Hipócrates, Calle Colón 4, Las Palmas (► 72)

Shopping

Despite Spain's membership of the European Union, the Canary Islands
have retained their special status as a free trade zone, with minimal import
duties and a low rate of value added tax (VAT) (4.5 per cent).

Many everyday items are considerably cheaper here than elsewhere.
Alcohol, tobacco, perfume, jewellery, clothing and electronic goods are all
sold cheaply at duty-free shops in Las Palmas and the south coast resorts.

Unlike elsewhere in the European Union, there are strict limits to the
amount of goods which can be exported for personal use. The allowances to
other European Union countries are 1 litre of spirits, 2 litres of wine and
either 200 cigarettes or 50 cigars.

Shopping Areas

- The biggest **range** of shops is found in Las Palmas, especially at the
  La Ballena and Las Arenas shopping malls and along Avenida Mesa
  y López, which has two branches of the leading Spanish department
  store El Corte Inglés.
- The **shopping centres** of Playa del Inglés are busy seven days a week, but
  the emphasis here is on price rather than quality.
- **Supermarkets** in all of the south coast resorts sell a wide range of local
  and imported food and drink.

Opening Times

- Most shops are open Monday to Saturday from around 10–1.30 and
  4.30–8.
- Some shops close on Saturday afternoon and most are closed on Sundays.
- The larger department stores and shopping malls in Las Palmas stay open
  throughout the day, while many shops in the south coast resorts are open
  daily 10–10.

Top Tips

- It is usual to **bargain** at markets and duty-free shops, where the price quoted may be about double what the shopkeeper is prepared to accept.
- Major **credit cards** are widely accepted.
- The **airport departure lounge** has an extensive shopping mall which is open throughout the night for last-minute purchases, though prices here are no better than elsewhere.

Canarian Classics

- For a good selection of **Canarian crafts** at reasonable prices, check out the Fedac shops in Las Palmas and Playa del Inglés.
- Local handicrafts are also available at the weekly **markets** which take place in various towns around the island.
- **Baskets and basketware** made out of woven palm fronds and banana leaves are manufactured in Ingenio and Teror.
- **Embroidered lace tablecloths** with geometric patterns are a speciality of Ingenio, Agüimes and San Bartolomé de Tirajana. They are sold at markets across the island and at the Museo de Piedras y Artesanía (handicrafts museum) in Ingenio.
- The bone-handled knives known as *naifes* were originally used by shepherds and workers in the banana plantations, but these days they have become a collector's item. Some of the patterns are remarkably intricate, with goathorn handles inlaid with brass. They are made in Santa María de Guía and sold in the Fedac shops in Las Palmas and Playa del Inglés.
- **Pottery** is still produced on Gran Canaria without the use of a wheel, just as it was in Guanche times (► 13). The main centres of production are La Atalaya, Hoya de Pineda and Lugarejos. In addition to everyday items such as ceramic bowls, jugs and plates, you can buy miniature versions of Guanche artefacts such as the Idol of Tara and jewellery based on the unique *pintaderas* (terracotta seals with geometric designs).
- Traditional **musical instruments** include the *timple* (a small four- or five-stringed guitar) and *chácaras* (castanets).
- If you want to take home some **Canarian music**, the best-known Canarian folk groups are Los Gofiones and Mestisay from Gran Canaria and Los Sabandeños from Tenerife.
- Other **popular souvenirs** include Canarian felt hats and miniature versions of Canarian wooden balconies.
- **Foods** which travel well include palm honey, *bienmesabe* (almond syrup), *mazapan* (almond cake), banana and cactus jam, dried herbs, almonds and jars of spicy *mojo* sauce (► 16).
- Other good buys are **coffee beans** from Agaete, **Canarian wine**, Arucas **rum**.
- Cuban-style **cigars** are produced on the nearby island of La Palma and are widely available on Gran Canaria.
- For something more healthy, **soap, shampoo and various skin lotions** are all produced on Gran Canaria from the juice of the aloe vera plant, which claims miraculous healing properties.

Best...

...for cheese:
Santiago Gil Romero, Santa María de Guía (► 101)
...for pastries:
Dulcería Nublo, Tejeda (► 120)
...for wine:
Bodeguilla Juananá, Puerto de Mogán (► 146)

Markets

- The two main **food markets** of Las Palmas, Mercado de Vegueta (► 66) and Mercado Central (► 74) are open six days a week from 8 am to 2 pm, as are the daily **covered markets** in Arucas and Gáldar.
- The following **weekly markets** offer a varied selection of fresh produce, local crafts, souvenirs, cheap clothes and household goods. Most of them start early and wind up by 2 pm.
- Arguineguín (Tue)
- Arucas (Sat)
- Gáldar (Thu)
- Moya (Sun)
- Puerto de Mogán (Fri)
- San Bartolomé de Tirajana (Sun)
- San Fernando, Maspalomas (Wed/Sat)
- San Nicolás de Tolentino (Sun)
- Teror (Sun)
- Vecindario (Wed)
- Vega de San Mateo (Sun)

Entertainment

Whatever your taste in entertainment, there is always something happening in Gran Canaria.

Las Palmas has a thriving arts and music scene, there are hundreds of discos and bars on the south coast, and there is always a local festival taking place somewhere on the island. In addition, hotels and tour operators in all the main resorts lay on a host of entertainments to keep their clients amused.

The best sources of information are local newspapers and tourist offices. If you have internet access, two useful sites for arts listings are www.canarynet.com and www.aicts.org. The weekend editions of *Canarias 7* and *La Provincia* carry full arts and entertainment listings.

Festivals and Folklore

- Traditional *fiestas* on Gran Canaria are colourful affairs. Most of them take place to mark a town or village saint's day, though the Christian element is combined with a heavy dose of pagan ritual dating back to pre-Hispanic times.
- The festivities tend to last for about a **week** and include stick fights, Canarian wrestling competitions (*lucha Canaria*) (► 25), bonfires, fireworks, folk dancing, street parties, children's parties, live bands and religious processions.
- **Carnival** (► 28) is celebrated across the island, though the biggest parades take place in Las Palmas.
- Details of **other festivals** are listed separately at the end of each chapter. Among the most interesting are Corpus Christi, Las Palmas in June (► 76), La Rama, Agaete in August (► 102), La Virgen de la Cuevita, Artenara in August (► 120), Fiesta del Charco, Puerto de la Aldea in September (► 149), Nuestra Señora del Rosario, Agüimes in October (► 149) and the pilgrimage to Nuestra SeñoraLa Virgen del Pino, Teror in September (► 102).

■ If you cannot get to a festival, you can still see **folk dancing** and hear **Canarian folk music** at the twice-weekly performances at the Pueblo Canario in Las Palmas (➤ 68).

Music

■ The main concert venues are the **Alfredo Kraus Auditorium** in Las Palmas, tel: 928 491770 (➤ 70) and the Las Tirajanas Auditorium in Maspalomas, tel: 928 172848 .

■ There are also various **outdoor music festivals** which take place in Las Palmas and on the coast. Check with tourist offices for detailed programmes, and keep an eye out for posters advertising concerts and special events.

Bars and Clubs

■ The busiest **nightlife** is concentrated in Las Palmas and Playa del Inglés. Playa del Inglés has a lively gay and lesbian scene, based around the Yumbo centre (➤ 148).

■ Nightlife in Gran Canaria starts late and goes on all night. Most **bars** in Las Palmas and the south coast resorts stay open until 2 am, while **discos** and **clubs** may not close until 6 am.

Casinos

■ There are two **casinos** in Gran Canaria. Casino Las Palmas (tel: 928 233908) is situated inside the Hotel Santa Catalina in Las Palmas (➤ 41), and Casino Tamarindos Palace (tel: 928 762724) in the Meliá Tamarindos in San Agustín.

Sport

The mild climate and warm seas make Gran Canaria a paradise for sports enthusiasts.

Watersports

Conditions for watersports are perfect throughout the year, with sea temperatures rarely dipping below 19°C and reaching an average of 23°C in September.

■ **Sailing** and **windsurfing** are best on the south coast, where a number of schools offer equipment hire and tuition.

■ **Beginners** should stick to the sheltered harbours of the southwest such as Puerto Rico and Puerto de Mogán, while **experienced** windsurfers enjoy the challenge of the southeast with its trade winds and strong waves.

■ The **sailing school** at Puerto Rico has produced several Olympic champions, and the world windsurfing championships have been held in Gran Canaria. There are two windsurfing schools: Surfcenter Dunkerbeck at Playa del Águila (tel: 928 762958) and Club Mistral Canarias, beside the aeroclub at nearby Playa de Tarajalillo (tel: 928 774025).

■ To see the **top windsurfers** in action, wait for the summer months when the wind speed reaches 60kph (Beaufort Scale 7) and the champion surfers come out to ride the huge waves at Pozo Izquierdo on the south-east coast.

■ **Surfing** with bodyboards is also popular, especially on Playa Las Canteras in Las Palmas (➤ 70) and along the north coast at San Andrés and Gáldar (➤ 98). In the south, two of the best spots are Playa de las Burras at San Agustín (➤ 159) and Playa de las Mujeres at Maspalomas (➤ 132). Boards can be hired at any of these beaches. The strongest waves are generally between September and March.

- **Scuba diving** is another popular activity, with the chance to see tropical fish, shipwrecks and underwater caves.
- There are fully certified **diving schools** in all the major resorts, with courses for beginners, children over eight years old, and more experienced divers. Most people start in the sheltered harbours of the south-west before moving on to the open sea.
- The best **dive location** on the island is the underwater nature reserve of El Cabrón off the east coast; other good spots are Sardina (► 98), La Isleta (Las Palmas) and Pasito Blanco. Some of the diving schools organise excursions to these places.
- If you don't want to scuba dive, most diving schools hire out **snorkelling** equipment.
- **Parascending**, **jet-skiing** and **water-skiing** are among the adrenalin rides on offer at the major south coast resorts. **Pedal boats** are also available for hire and make a good way of getting out on the water with younger children.
- **Swimming** is possible throughout the year because of the warm sea temperature. The beaches of the south coast are generally calm but as this is the Atlantic Ocean conditions can change rapidly and you need to keep a close eye on children.
- The major **beaches** have lifeguards and safety flags; a red flag indicates that swimming is dangerous.
- Most hotels and apartment blocks have **swimming pools** and many have a separate pool for children.

Outdoor Activities

- **Fishing** trips can be arranged from the harbour at Puerto Rico (► 142), though there is also good rod fishing from the jetties and harbour walls at ports such as Puerto de la Aldea and Puerto de Mogán.
- Fishing in the **inland reservoirs** is only allowed with a licence; for details, enquire at your nearest tourist office.
- **Golf** is growing in popularity, with golfers from northern Europe fleeing frost and winter greens for Gran Canaria's year-round spring climate. Until recently there were just two courses on Gran Canaria, but now there are five and more are under construction. The oldest golf club in Spain, Real Club de Golf de Las Palmas (► 102), is based at Caldera de Bandama and there are also courses at Maspalomas, El Salobre and Telde. A second course is being built at El Salobre, and new courses at Tauro and Las Meloneras will take the total to eight by 2002.
- **Walking** in the mountains has been made easier by the restoration of the network of *caminos reales* (royal roads), medieval footpaths which were once the main routes across the island. Conditions in the mountains can be very different from on the coast and it is important to be prepared, even in summer, with strong shoes, warm clothing, food, water and a good map.

Spectator Sports

- **Football** is played at the Estadio Insular in Las Palmas, where UD Las Palmas take on the top Spanish teams in the Primera Liga between September and June. The most keenly anticipated matches are those against local rivals Tenerife.
- *Lucha canaria* (Canarian wrestling) bouts (► 25) are held most weeks at arenas across the island. For details, ask at tourist offices or check the fixtures in the local newspapers.
- *Vela Latina* (lateen sailing) regattas take place along the seafront in Las Palmas at weekends between April and October (► 76).

Las Palmas

Getting Your Bearings

Crowded, cosmopolitan and teeming with expectation, Las Palmas is the only place in the Canary Islands with that big-city feel. Like any big city, it has its problems with pollution, traffic and crime; but like any big city it also has its compensations, such as good restaurants and shops and a vibrant cultural life. From the museums and historic houses of Vegueta to the bustle of the modern city down by the port, Las Palmas has it all.

Las Palmas stretches out like a long, thin lizard along the island's northeastern tip. The shape of the city has the effect of making it seem even larger than it is; from the old town to the modern centre is a distance of more than 5km.

The easiest way to tackle Las Palmas is to break it down into manageable districts, and to travel between them by bus. Head straight for Vegueta, the oldest part, with cobbled streets, shady squares and colonial-style architecture. It was founded by the conqueror Juan Rejón in 1478 on a *vegueta* (meadow) of *las palmas* (palm trees) beside the Guiniguada ravine.

Triana, adjoining Vegueta, has a pleasing mix of buildings from the 16th to 20th centuries, together with theatres, lively shopping streets and open-air bars. North of Parque San Telmo, the long route through various residential districts leads to Parque Santa Catalina, the hub of the modern city. Playa de las Canteras, which must be one of the finest city beaches in the world, is a short walk away. Beyond Puerto de la Luz, Spain's largest port, lie the volcanic peaks of La Isleta, providing a scenic backdrop. Although it is now connected to the mainland

Preceding page: Yachts in the marina at Las Palmas

Below: Playa de las Canteras was Gran Canaria's first beach resort

Right: A Modernist café kiosk in Parque San Telmo

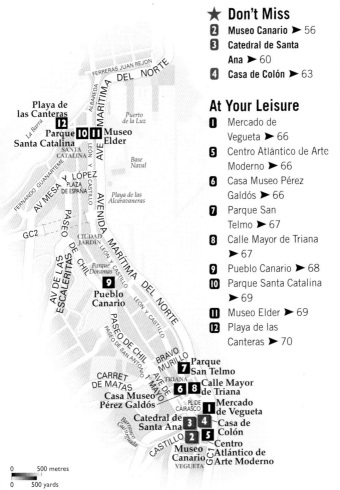

by a port built on land reclaimed from the sea, until the 19th century La Isleta was an island, cut off twice a day by high tide.

The distances involved mean this is not really a city for walking, with one magnificent exception – the Avenida Marítima along the seafront. As you stroll along the promenade, with ferries, tankers, cruise ships, navy vessels, yachts and lateen sailboats heading in and out of the port, you appreciate Las Palmas' historic role as a maritime city and a crossroads of continents and cultures.

Explore the best of both old and new Las Palmas with a morning of historic sights and an afternoon of entertainment.

Las Palmas in a Day

9.00 am

Spend some time walking around the Vegueta and soak up the old town atmosphere. Except for on Sundays, visit the **Mercado de Vegueta** (➤ 66), where the locals do their shopping. Then head for the fascinating **Museo Canario** (➤ 56) to learn about the earliest inhabitants of the island, the Guanches.

11.00 am

Look into the peaceful courtyard of the **Catedral de Santa Ana** (➤ 60, left). Follow this with a visit to the **Casa de Colón** (➤ 63), where you can explore the history of Las Palmas (below, gargoyle on the wall of the Casa).

Noon

Go to the **Centro Atlantico de Arte Moderno** (➤ 66) to see contemporary art representative of Las Palmas and Canarian life. Then, after all that sightseeing, relax with an apéritif at one of the terrace cafés in Plaza de Cairasco or a spot of window-shopping in the streets around **Calle Mayor de Triana** (➤ 67).

1.00 pm

Head for **Casa Montsedeoca** (➤ 71) for a lunchtime table in the courtyard. If you feel like something more down-to-earth, **El Herreño** (➤ 71) serves great tapas.

2.30 pm

Take a No 1 bus from Parque San Telmo for the journey downtown.
On the way, get off at the **Pueblo Canario** (► 68) and a look at this
amazing Canarian "village" in the middle of the city. Canarian folk-dancing
(above) takes place at 11.30 am on Sunday and 5.30 pm on Thursday. Hop
back on the No 1 bus again and get off at Calle Alfredo L Jones, between
Parque Santa Catalina (► 69) and Playa de las Canteras.

4.00 pm

Head for Parque Santa Catalina and a ride
on the *Guagua Turística* tour bus (► 69) before
enjoying the hands-on activities at the **Museo Elder**
(► 69) in Parque Santa Catalina. Alternatively,
if you feel like you've done enough sightseeing,
relax on the
beach at
**Playa de
las Canteras**

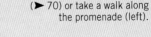

(► 70) or take a walk along
the promenade (left).

7.30 pm

Take a taxi up to La Isleta for
an evening meal at **El Padrino**
(► 71) and views over the city,
with the lights sparkling below.

❷

Museo Canario

If you only see one museum in Gran Canaria, this should be the one. It provides a fascinating introduction to the culture and lifestyle of the earliest Canarios, who have come to be known as the Guanches. As well as glimpses into their daily life, the museum also offers a remarkable collection of complete preserved mummies, whose discovery has provided a link between the Guanches and the ancient Egyptians.

The museum was founded in 1879 by Dr Gregorio Chil, based on his own private collection. At first it was housed in rented premises in the old city hall, but when Dr Chil died in 1901, he bequeathed his collection to the city, along with his home. The museum moved to its present site in 1923 and with the removal of its natural science collection it is now almost totally devoted to archaeology and the lives of the Guanche inhabitants of Gran Canaria between 500 BC and AD 1500.

The exhibits are ranged over 11 galleries on two floors and it makes sense to follow them in order. It is best to allow at least an hour. The first room, **The Habitat**, has scale reproductions of Guanche dwellings, including a stone house from Telde and a cave village. Although

The Guanche Trail

If the Museo Canario has given you a taste for Guanche culture and history, you can learn more by visiting these sights:

- Barranco de Guayadeque (➤ 126)
- Cenobio de Valerón (➤ 90)
- Cuatro Puertas (➤ 95)
- Mundo Aborigen (➤ 140)
- Roque Bentaiga (➤ 110)

the Guanches are popularly thought of as cavemen, they actually lived in a variety of houses, including natural caves, artificial caves and stone-built houses that had stone or thatched roofs.

Passing through a small corridor devoted to stonework, where tools such as axes and millstones are displayed, next is a gallery dedicated to the **Guanche economy**. The aboriginal people kept pigs and goats, grew and ground barley, harvested shellfish and made jewellery out of conch shells, all of which is brought to life through a series of realistic tableaux.

Archaeologists are searching for links between the Guanches and ancient Egyptians

The next room is devoted to **magic and religion**, two areas of Guanche culture which are unlikely ever to be fully understood. The accounts of the first invaders suggest that the Guanches worshipped a deity called Alcorán, and that their religion centred on rain-making and fertility. This is reinforced by some of the idols in this room, vivid terracotta figures incorporating human and animal features with explicit depictions of female genitalia. The best-known is the **Idol of Tara**, a red ochre figure with exaggerated breasts, possibly symbolising the earth goddess.

The geometric designs which were widely used by the Guanches may also have had a religious function, with circles representing the sun and triangles the earth, sea and sky. Here also is a reproduction of the *Cueva Pintada* (Painted Cave) at **Gáldar** (► 98), with red and black murals of geometric shapes such as circles, spirals, triangles, zigzags and squares. There is also a large collection of *pintaderas*, terracotta or wooden seals with intricate geometric motifs which may have decorated the skin like a tattoo, or painted property as a mark of ownership.

The second floor displays begin on the **balcony**, with clothing and other objects made out of leather and vegetable fibres. The tanning of goatskin and pigskin was clearly advanced, and the Guanches also wove intricate baskets and mats out of palm fronds, just as the people of Gran Canaria do today.

Just off from here is the most compelling and macabre section, dealing with **death and mummification** – a practice which the Guanches may have learned from the ancient Egyptians. When Guanche people died, their bodies were washed in the sea,

Fertility symbols were a common feature of pre-Hispanic culture on Gran Canaria

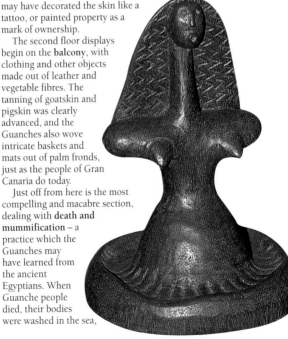

their internal organs were removed and the corpse was left to dry in the sun. It was then wrapped in a shroud made of leather or rush matting and placed inside a cave on planks of wood so that it did not come into contact with the earth. One of the galleries features a reproduction burial cave, and several complete mummies are on display. Some of the mummies are as much as 1.83m tall, reinforcing the idea that the Guanches were an exceptionally tall race.

The walls of this gallery are lined with rows of **Cro-Magnon skulls**. A few of them are shown to have survived a primitive form of trepanning, a surgical operation in which incisions were made in the skull to treat victims of battle injuries and diseases such as epilepsy.

Guanche pottery used geometric designs

The final galleries feature examples of **pre-Hispanic pottery** and its links to pottery-making techniques on Gran Canaria today. The pottery was made without the use of a potter's wheel, using bones, shells and bamboo sticks to shape the clay. Once again the familiar geometric shapes appear, painted in red ochre to create striking patterns. Similar pieces of pottery are still being produced in the village of La Atalaya (➤ 83).

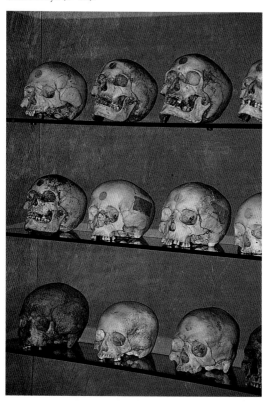

The rows of skulls make a grisly sight

Some of the mummies found on Gran Canaria

Luigi de Cadamosto, a Venetian explorer, said in 1455: "The sons of Gran Canaria are cunning sharp, they can leap over wide abysses with the greatest of agility and can throw a stone with such sure aim that they never miss the target."

TAKING A BREAK

Café del Real (Calle Dr Chil 19), around the corner from the museum, serves coffee, sandwiches and light lunches.

🕂 183 E1
✉ Calle Dr Verneau 2
☎ 928 315600
🕔 Mon–Fri 10–8, Sat–Sun 10–2
🚌 1 to Teatro Pérez Galdós; 2, 3 to Alameda de Colón
💷 Inexpensive

MUSEO CANARIO: INSIDE INFO

Top tips The captions are all in Spanish, but the museum shop sells a guidebook with English translations and there are occasional **guided tours** in English. These usually take place on Tuesday and Friday at 11 am.
• The **shop** sells a good selection of books about the Canary Islands and also has Guanche-related artefacts. The most popular item is a pottery reproduction of the Idol of Tara.

Hidden gem Don't miss the collection of **old maps** in the reading room, some of which date back to the time of Columbus.

In more depth The museum has a **library and historical archive** containing more than 40,000 items. It is open Monday to Friday 10–8.

❸

Catedral de Santa Ana

The largest church in the Canary Islands dominates the Vegueta skyline and looks down over a handsome square from its impressive neo-classical façade. Begun in 1497, it took more than 400 years to complete, with the result that it is a curious and eclectic blend of Gothic, Renaissance, baroque and neo-classical styles.

Unless you are arriving for a service, you will enter through the **Patio de los Naranjos** (Courtyard of the Orange Trees), just around the corner from the main entrance on the square. This beautiful cloister is built in late 16th-century Canarian style and has wooden galleries along two of its sides. Notice the ceramic plaque dedicated to the bishops of the Canary Islands who have served in America, an indication of the close links between the Canaries and Spain's Latin American colonies over the past 500 years.

Also in the courtyard, the **Museo Diocesano** (Diocesan Museum) is devoted to religious art. A staircase leads to the **Sala Capitular** (chapter-house), with a hand-made ceramic tiled floor, unique in the Canary Islands, and sculptures by Luján Pérez (a well-known Canarian artist). The other galleries have paintings and furniture,

Five centuries of contact between the Canaries and America

The cathedral has been restored to its former glory

Left: The Patio de los Naranjos

including an 18th-century throne by Canarian goldsmith José Eugenio.

A 16th-century doorway, Puerta del Aire, leads to the **main cathedral**. After a recent restoration, the interior is full of light and space, and the grey basalt columns of the original Gothic structure are shining once again. There are three naves of equal height, and side chapels containing the tombs of various bishops, as well as the poet Bartolomé Cairasco (1538–1610), the historian José de Viera y Clavijo (1731–1813) and the diplomat Fernando de León y Castillo (1842–1918), whose grandiloquent tomb lists his many titles and records his wish to be buried among his people in Gran Canaria. The figures of saints beneath the dome were sculpted by Luján Pérez, the artist responsible for remodelling the cathedral façade in the late 19th century.

A separate ticket gives access to the **cathedral tower**. A lift takes you up to the viewing platform but you can climb to the top of the tower for even better views. From here you look down over Plaza de Santa Ana, the main square of the old town, with its bronze dogs, lampstands, palm trees and Renaissance mansions.

During the **feast of Corpus Christi** in June (► 76), the Plaza de Santa Ana becomes a carpet of flowers and participants throw rose-petals from their balconies as a procession moves out of the cathedral and around the streets of the old town.

Climb the tower for views over the rooftops

TAKING A BREAK

The pavement cafés of **Plaza de Cairasco** are perfect for people-watching and are situated a short walk from the cathedral, across the main road which separates Vegueta from Triana.

➕ 183 E1
✉ Plaza de Santa Ana (entrance at Calle Espíritu Santo 20)
☎ 928 313600
🕐 Mon–Fri 10–4.30, Sat 10–1.30
🚌 1 to Teatro Pérez Galdós; 2, 3 to Alameda de Colón
🎟 Inexpensive

CATEDRAL DE SANTA ANA: INSIDE INFO

Top tip You can get into the cathedral for **free** by going to Mass on Sunday morning – though the museum and Patio de los Naranjos will be off limits.

Hidden gem Look out for the *Stations of the Cross* by Jésus Arencibia, a remarkable series of black-and-white drawings completed in the 1960s and exhibited in the gallery nearest to the courtyard entrance.

One to miss Once you have seen the Sala Capitular, you could afford to miss the rest of the **Museo Diocesano** if you are in a hurry.

4

Casa de Colón

Pass through the heavy doors of one of the oldest houses in Las Palmas and you enter a cool courtyard, with dark wooden balconies surrounding a Renaissance patio and a pair of noisy parrots standing guard over an ancient stone well. If Christopher Columbus ever set foot in Las Palmas then he almost certainly stayed in this house. Historians still differ over the precise movements of the explorer, but most agree that he called in at Las Palmas on his way to discover Cuba during his first voyage to the New World in 1492. If so, he would have presented his credentials and been given lodging at the military governor's residence, one of the first buildings to be completed in Las Palmas following the Spanish Conquest of 1478.

Did Christopher Columbus sleep here?

Whatever the truth about Columbus, this house, the Casa de Colón (Colón means Columbus to Canarians) is worth a visit as it is one of the finest examples of traditional Canarian architecture, with carved stone portals, balconies and richly ornamented façades. It has been turned into a museum dedicated to Columbus, despite a lack of personal possessions of the great explorer, linking together his voyages, the history of the Canary Islands and their role as a bridge between Europe and America.

If you only have time for a short visit, the **ground-floor rooms** offer the most interesting material on Columbus and his

voyages. Among the nautical charts, navigational instruments and model boats, look out for the following:

• a reconstruction of Columbus' **cabin** on board the caravel *Santa Maria*
• the **log book** of Columbus' first voyage to the New World, with an entry recording how he called in at Las Palmas for repairs
• the **seals of the Treaty of Tordesillas** (1494), which divided the undiscovered Atlantic into Spanish and Portuguese spheres of influence
• the **map** of the known world in 1500 by Spanish cartographer Juan de la Cosa, who accompanied Columbus on his early voyages, which included those parts of America discovered by Columbus but left large parts of the continent out.

Christopher Columbus – a Spanish hero born in Italy

The **upstairs galleries** contain exhibits on the history of Las Palmas as well as a collection of 16th- to 20th-century paintings on loan from the Prado Museum in Madrid.

Wooden balconies are a feature of traditional Canarian houses

Above: Children
enjoy the model
ships and
medieval maps

Right:
Columbus made
three visits to
Gran Canaria

Stepping Stone

Because of the trade winds that
favour sea voyages to the west,
the Canaries have often been
used as a stepping stone
between Europe and America.

EL GRAN NAVEGANTE CRISTOBAL COLÓN
HIZO ESCALA EN GRAN CANARIA
EN EL PRIMERO (1492), SEGUNDO(1493) Y CUARTO (1502)
DE SUS VIAJES AL NUEVO CONTINENTE.
ESTA CASA, QUE TRADICIONALMENTE LLEVÓ SU NOMBRE,
GUARDA EL RECUERDO DE LA ESTANCIA DEL ALMIRANTE
EN LAS PALMAS DE GRAN CANARIA
JUNIO. 28. 1993.

TAKING A BREAK

For lunch, try the Canarian tapas at **El Herreño** (► 71) or the
wacky décor and vegetarian cuisine at **Hipócrates** (► 72).

➕ 183 E1 ✉ Calle Colón 1 ☎ 928 312386 🕐 Mon–Fri 9–7 (9–2 in Aug),
Sat–Sun 9–3 🚌 1 to Teatro Pérez Galdós; 2, 3 to Alameda de Colón 🎫 Free

CASA DE COLÓN: INSIDE INFO

Hidden gem The **crypt** is devoted to objects from the pre-Colombian period,
showing the richness of the various American cultures before he arrived. Among
the artefacts on display are Ecuadorean fertility symbols dating back to 500 BC,
replicas of Aztec and Mayan pottery, and basketware from the 20th-century
"pre-Colombian" Yanomani Indians of Brazil.

One to miss If you are in a hurry, the **Prado collection** contains little that is
exceptional, apart from some etchings by Goya and a *Virgin and Child* by Luis de
Menéndez.

At Your Leisure

4 Mercado de Vegueta

A visit to Las Palmas' oldest market is a good way to appreciate the variety of fresh produce available on Gran Canaria. This is where the locals do their shopping and it is busy from early in the morning. Stalls around the outer aisles sell Atlantic fish such as *sama* and *cherne* as well as octopus, squid and sole. Greengrocers sell local bananas, tomatoes, potatoes, mangoes, avocados and figs. Other stalls specialise in Canarian cheeses, such as *queso de flor* from Guía and goat's cheese from Fuerteventura, with its paprika-coated rind.

All around the market are stand-up tapas bars and *churrerías*, where people come after doing their shopping to dip *churros* (dough fritters) into mugs of coffee or chocolate – don't miss Churrería Mayda, which has been making *churros* since 1948. The market used to be known as the "market of the forty thieves", ostensibly because of the number of stalls.

🚑 183 E1 ✉ Corner of Plaza del Mercado and Calle Mendizábal 🕐 Mon–Sat 8–2 🚌 1 to Teatro Pérez Galdós

5 Centro Atlántico de Arte Moderno (CAAM)

Step behind the 18th-century façade of a typical old Vegueta house and you enter this bright, modern art museum, with sparkling white walls and a glass-covered rooftop terrace. Opened in 1989, the museum has become a focal point of contemporary cultural life in Las Palmas. There is a rolling programme of temporary exhibitions, but the emphasis is on Canarian art and the relationship between the Atlantic cultures of Europe, Africa and America. The museum has a separate gallery in Plaza de San Antonio Abad, near the Casa de Colón, which acts as a showcase for exhibitions of work by young Canarian artists.

🚑 183 E1 ✉ Calle de los Balcones 9 ☎ 928 311824 🕐 Tue–Sat 10–9, Sun 10–2 🚌 1 to Teatro Pérez Galdós; 2, 3 to Alameda de Colón 🎟 Free

6 Casa Museo Pérez Galdós

This typical Canarian, 18th-century home was the birthplace of Benito Pérez Galdós (1843–1920), the Canary Islands' greatest novelist and a leading exponent of Spanish

A wide variety of fresh fish is available at the Mercado de Vegueta

Take the children to play in Parque San Telmo

Realism who has been compared to Balzac and Dickens. His best-known work is *Episodios Nacionales*, a vivid portrait of 19th-century Spain. Although he left Las Palmas at the age of 19 and never returned, the islanders are extremely proud of Pérez Galdós and the house has been turned into a museum devoted to his life and work. It contains mementoes of his life from his cradle (he was the youngest of ten children) to his death mask, as well as manuscripts, furniture and reproductions of his bedroom and study from Madrid and Santander. Don't miss the statue of Pérez Galdós in the courtyard – a copy of which stands on top of the bus station in Parque San Telmo.

🖿 183 E2 ✉ Calle Cano 6 ☎ 928 366976 🕐 Mon–Fri 9–8, Sat 10–6, Sun 10–3 (tours on the hour) 🚌 1, 11, 15, 41 to Parque San Telmo 🎟 Free

7 Parque San Telmo
The most appealing of all Las Palmas' parks, this is the one most people see first as they step out of the bus station. There are palm trees giving plenty of shade, benches and a children's playground, but the main attractions are the bandstand at the centre and the Modernist (Spanish art-nouveau) café inside a pavilion decorated with ceramic tiles. The café is open during daylight hours. The park was initially built on the site of a small cove but the bus station and motorway have forced the sea to recede. The chapel in the southwest corner is dedicated to sailors and fishermen, with model boats hanging from the coffered ceiling.

Near here is the military headquarters where General Franco launched the Civil War in 1936; a plaque marks the spot where he announced his rebellion "for the salvation of Spain".

🖿 183 E3 🚌 1, 11, 15, 41

8 Calle Mayor de Triana
This was the first street in Las Palmas to be pedestrianised in the 1970s and it has become a popular place to take a stroll. The best time to come is during the early-evening *paseo* (around 6–8), when people spill on

Four Top Monuments
- Sculpture of Guanche pole-vaulter, in the gardens of Hotel Santa Catalina (➤ 41)
- Bust of Christopher Columbus, Alameda de Colón
- Monument to Pérez Galdós, Plaza de la Feria
- Monument to Canarian farmers, Plaza de España

The folk dancing displays at the Pueblo Canario are always popular – get there early if you want a seat

to the streets and buskers entertain the crowds.

Until recently Las Palmas' principal shopping street, it is most notable for its range of architectural styles, with several shopfronts in Modernist (Spanish art-nouveau) style. Although the biggest stores have now moved elsewhere, this is still a pleasant area for shopping, with craft shops and arty boutiques in the surrounding streets.

➕ 183 E2 🚌 1, 11, 15, 41 to Parque San Telmo

❾ Pueblo Canario

This "village" of traditional Canarian buildings in the heart of a modern city may seem like a tourist trap, but it was designed as exactly the

opposite, a serious attempt to preserve Canarian culture and architecture before tourism wiped them out. There is nothing artificial about the enthusiastic displays of folk dancing, which take place twice a week in front of an appreciative and largely Spanish audience. The women wear white bodices and long flowing dresses, the men embroidered waistcoats, white skirts and socks around the knees, and the songs vary from jaunty to melancholy, with a strong hint of the Caribbean.

The complex was designed by the Modernist artist Néstor Martín Fernández de la Torre (1887–1938), whose work is on display in the Museo Néstor. Among the highlights are his epic cycles *Poema del Atlántico* (*Atlantic Poem*), in which the sea is interwoven with scenes from ancient mythology, and the unfinished *Poema*

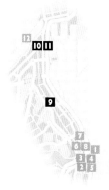

de la Tierra (*Earth Poem*), blending themes of erotic love with studies of native Canarian plants.

➕ 183 D5 ✉ Parque Doramas
🎭 Folk dancing: Sun 11.30 am, Thu 5.30 pm 🚌 1, 15, 41 💶 Free (Café and restaurant moderate)

Museo Néstor

➕ 183 D5 ☎ 928 245135 🕐 Tue–Fri 10–1 , 4–8, Sun 11–2 💶 Inexpensive

⑩ Parque Santa Catalina

This large open space, more like a plaza than a park, is the nearest thing this sprawling city has to a centre. With cafés, news-stands, playgrounds and shops, the square is busy day and night. This is where you can most feel the cosmopolitan atmosphere of Las Palmas, as tourists mingle with sailors, shoeshine boys, hustlers, African traders, and the old men who play dominoes and chess beneath the palm trees.

During the day, the whole area becomes a cut-price bazaar, with Chinese, Indian and Russian shops selling electronic goods from the duty-free port. The plaza is also home to the Museo Elder and the starting-point for the *Guagua Turística* tour bus (► 38).

➕ 182 B4 🚌 1, 2, 3

The locals gather to play games at the café tables in Parque Santa Catalina

⑪ Museo Elder

The slogan of this science museum, which opened in 1999, is "*Tocar por favor*" ("Please do touch"). Of 200 exhibits, all but a handful are interactive and visitors are encouraged to pull levers and push buttons to their heart's content. This is a great place to take the children, but be warned that those with an inquisitive nature may never want to leave.

The most fun is on the first floor, with exhibits relating to mathematics, magnetism and the human body – move pieces around a chess set, solve mathematical riddles, blow up a hot-air balloon and work out your weight on the moon before coming to grips with the world's largest magic square.

Three Top Joyrides

- *Bahia Cat* (Expensive): a one-hour cruise around the port from the Muelle Deportivo marina (Mon–Thu 11 am and 3.30 pm, Fri–Sat 3.30 pm and 1 am.)
- *Ciclo Feliz* (Moderate): "happy bikes" for families can be hired on the seafront promenade by taking the underpass behind the bus station on Parque San Telmo.
- *Guagua Turística* (Moderate): this open-top tour bus (► 38) leaves Parque Santa Catalina at regular intervals throughout the day.

The Museo Elder adds a modern touch to Las Palmas' main square

Adults and older children may also enjoy the ground-floor displays on transport and astronomy, with cars and planes to test out. There is also a large-screen Imax cinema with films in English and an open-air terrace café with views over Parque Santa Catalina and the port.

➕ 182 B4 ✉ Parque Santa Catalina
☎ 828 011828 🕐 Tue–Sun 10–8 in winter, 11–10 in summer 🚌 1, 2, 3
💰 Moderate (IMAX cinema extra)

🔢 Playa de las Canteras

The popular Playa de las Canteras offers more than 3km of golden sand set in a sheltered bay and protected by

a natural rock barrier which breaks the waves and turns the sea into a warm, shallow lagoon at low tide.

Long before the south coast was developed, this was the first tourist resort in Gran Canaria, and the bucket-and-spade atmosphere survives, along the wide promenade, with its ice-cream parlours, beach shops and Italian cafés.

At the western end of the beach, where the reef runs out, surfers ride the waves in front of the Auditorio Alfredo Kraus, a mosque-like building constructed out of volcanic rock by the Catalan architect Oscar Tusquets. The auditorium, which opened in 1997, is named after the Canarian tenor Alfredo Kraus (1927–1999), who gave one of his last recitals here.

➕ 182 A4 🚌 1, 2, 3, 20, 21, 22

For Kids

The top family attraction is the **Museo Elder** (➤ 69), though older children might enjoy the model boats at the **Casa de Colón** (➤ 63) and the rows of ghoulish skulls at the **Museo Canario** (➤ 56). There are **playgrounds** in all the parks, and the beach at **Playa de las Canteras** (➤ 70) is very child-friendly. The rides on a "happy bike" or the open-top *Guagua Turística* (➤ 38) are also ideal for children.

Where to...
Eat and Drink

Prices
Expect to pay per person for a meal, excluding drinks and service
£ under 12 Euros ££ 12–24 Euros £££ over 24 Euros

Most restaurants on Gran Canaria are open throughout the year, though they may close for an annual holiday, usually in August.

Café Santa Catalina £

This pleasant, open-air café is situated on Las Palmas' central square, where the old men gather to play chess and dominoes beneath the palms. With wicker chairs on a shady terrace, it makes a good place to while away some time reading the papers, writing your postcards or just watching the world go by. The lunch menu is Italian-influenced, featuring pasta, pizza and salads, but most people just come for an ice-cream or a coffee and a pastry.

➕ 182 B4 ⊠ Parque Santa Catalina
🕔 Daily 10 am–1 am

Casa Montesdeoca ££–£££

The most elegant restaurant in Las Palmas is situated in a 16th-century town house, built by the Jewish Montes de Oca family, who gave their name to the street. The bar, with its old portraits and hanging hams, is a good place to meet but you should really try to get a table in the patio beneath the trees. The service is formal and over-attentive at times, making it difficult to relax, but the cooking is first-class. The menu features Canarian and Spanish dishes with an emphasis on fish, and there is a good selection of both local and Spanish wines.

➕ 183 E1 ⊠ Calle Montesdeoca 10
🕔 928 333466 🕔 Mon–Sat 1–4, 8–11.30

Don Quijote II ££

Unwind from a shopping trip at this do-it-yourself restaurant, where the speciality is *carne a la piedra*, meat cooked at the table on a hot stone. There's steak, chicken or pork and the waiter brings you a plate of raw meat. The meat comes with French fries, a big bowl of salad and a selection of relishes including beetroot, red cabbage and *allioli* (garlic mayonnaise). Bottles of Rioja are put out on the table but there is also an extensive wine list.

El Herreño £–££

Hanging hams in the bar and a large brick oven give this place a rustic feel, enhanced by the buzz of conversation and the bustle of the white-shirted waiters. It is situated in the courtyard of an old house just around the corner from the Mercado de Vegueta. The owner is from El Hierro, one of the Canary Islands, and so naturally the menu features traditional Canary Islands cooking, accompanied by local wine. The house special is roast pork with a handful of roast potatoes, which makes an excellent lunch-time snack.

➕ 182 A3 ⊠ Calle Olof Palme 36
(near Plaza de España) 🕔 928 227847
🕔 Daily 1–4, 8–midnight

El Padrino ££

Drive to the end of the road on La Isleta – or take bus 41 – to reach

➕ 183 E1 ⊠ Calle Mendizábal 5
🕔 928 310513 🕔 Daily
10.30 am–1 am

this celebrated fish restaurant. The people of Las Palmas come here at weekends and they know a good thing when they see one. Most of the tables are out of doors, in a large greenhouse beside the car-park which can get stiflingly hot in summer. The crusty bread comes straight out of the oven and is served with a bowl of *allioli* (garlic mayonnaise). Almost everything on the menu is fishy, including seafood flown in from Galicia as well as the local catch. The menu contains a list of the day's suggestions and it is probably worth heeding their advice.

➕ 179 E5 ✉ Calle Jesús Nazareno 1, Las Coloradas ☎ 928 462094 🕒 Daily 1–4, 8–11

Hipócrates ££

Vegetarians can have a hard time in Gran Canaria, but this place is a treat, serving fresh, inventive vegetarian cuisine in a town house opposite the interesting Casa de Colón (▲ 63). The décor is bright and airy, the service is friendly and the cooking is far from dull. Salads are a work of art, piled high with tropical fruit and dressed with olive oil and soya sauce. The desserts might include fresh papaya in liqueur. There is a good selection of herb teas and fresh fruit juices but you can also have beer or wine with your meal.

➕ 183 E1 ✉ Calle Colón 4 ☎ 928 311171 🕒 Mon 8.30 pm–midnight; Tue–Sat 1–4, 8.30–midnight; Sun 1–4

Hotel Madrid £

The tables on the square outside this historic hotel (▲ 41) are the perfect place for an early-evening drink, accompanied by a plate of *papas arrugadas* (spicy potatoes) or pork crackling rolled in *gofio*. Although most people come here for a snack before moving on elsewhere, the bar also serves reasonably priced set meals at lunchtime and in the evening.

➕ 183 E2 ✉ Plaza de Cairasco 4 ☎ 928 360664 🕒 Daily 10 am–1 am

La Dolce Vita ££

This intimate little trattoria with exposed brick arches and white-washed walls is hidden away in the back streets of the old town. The walls are covered with film posters and portraits of Italian film stars such as Sophia Loren. The cooking is authentic Italian, featuring fresh pasta dishes with several vegetarian options as well as a selection of antipasti (cheese, salami, grilled vegetables) designed for sharing. Desserts are home-made and delicious, and there is an all-Italian wine list.

➕ 183 E1 ✉ Calle Agustín Millares 15 ☎ 928 310643 🕒 Mon–Sat 1.30–4, 9–midnight

La Strada £

This large, bustling self-service restaurant is set just back from the beach, making it popular with local families enjoying a day out. There are few frills but this is just the place for big appetites or anyone on a budget wanting one good-value meal a day. The food just keeps on coming – cold meat, seafood, salads, paella, omelettes, hot dishes – and you can eat as much as you like for a set price. The dessert buffet features a range of fresh fruit as well as baked bananas and ice-cream.

➕ 182 B3 ✉ Calle Tomás Miller 58 ☎ 928 273351 🕒 Daily noon–11

O'Sole Mio ££

With outdoor tables beneath huge parasols on one of Las Palmas' most attractive squares, this Italian pizzeria buzzes on summer evenings. The menu features steaks, fish and pasta dishes but most people settle for a pizza, cooked the proper Italian way in a wood-fired brick oven. Choose from classic flavours like mozzarella and tomato or roasted aubergine and parmesan, or try your luck with a novelty "African pizza", with banana and pineapple.

➕ 183 E2 ✉ Plaza de Cairasco 3 ☎ 928 383746 🕒 Daily 1–4, 8–11

Where to...
Shop

The focus of shopping in Las Palmas has gradually shifted away from the old town and towards the port.

The specialist shops are still to be found in Vegueta and in the streets around Calle Mayor de Triana, but the upmarket fashion boutiques have moved downtown to the smarter Avenida Mesa y López district.

Between here and the port, the area around Parque Santa Catalina resembles an Oriental bazaar, with numerous Indian-run shops selling cheap cameras, watches, cigars, clothes and electronic goods on streets such as Calle Tomás Miller, Calle Luis Morote and Calle Alfredo L Jones.

In most of these shops you are expected to **bargain** and you should be able to pick up a good deal if you can haggle well.

SHOPPING CENTRES

The local people do their shopping at the huge **shopping** centres which sprang up on the edge of the city in the 1990s.

These giant malls are a mixture of shopping and entertainment, with multiplex cinemas, restaurants and pubs open well into the night, in addition to high-street chains.

The biggest centre is **La Ballena**, 3km out of town on the road to Teror. This has a hypermarket and more than 100 shops, including Benetton, Yves Rocher, López and The Disney Store.

A second shopping centre, **Las Arenas**, is situated at the west end of Las Canteras beach, facing the Auditorio Alfredo Kraus and close to one of the stops for the *Guagua Turística* tour bus.

AVENIDA MESA Y LÓPEZ

This wide avenue, with a laurel-shaded promenade at its centre, is the principal shopping street of Las Palmas.

At the top of the promenade, **Plaza de España** (also known as Plaza de la Victoria) is a busy roundabout with a monument at its centre, dedicated to Canarian farmers and mothers.

This popular meeting-place is where supporters of **UD Las Palmas** football team gather to celebrate their team's victories.

Department Store

This is where you will find **El Corte Inglés**, the biggest department store on the island, whose two branches face one another on opposite sides of the street. Whether you are after leather or suede, perfume or pearls, you will probably be able to find it here.

The main store, on the northern side, has four floors of fashions for women, men, children and teenagers, a supermarket in the basement and the **Club del Gourmet**, featuring Canarian and Spanish food and wines. The top-floor café is a good place for a break when you've had enough shopping.

The second shop across the street sells **books**, **music**, **electronic goods**, **household items and souvenirs**. A restaurant on the top floor serves Canarian cuisine. Both stores are open Monday to Saturday, 10–10.

Fashion and Designer Boutiques

The rest of Avenida Mesa Y López is mostly devoted to fashion and designer boutiques. Among the well-known names here are **Benetton**, **Massimo Dutti** (fashion), **López** (shoes and leather goods), **Prénatal** (babies' and children's clothes), **Osh Kosh B'Gosh** (children's fashion), **Pronovias** (ballgowns and wedding dresses), **Zara** (fashion) and the **Body Shop** (cosmetics).

TRIANA

Calle Mayor de Triana (▶ 67) is no longer the smartest shopping street in town, but it is still the best place for a *paseo* combined with a spot of window-shopping. There are one or two high-street names here, such as **Benetton** and **Mango**, but it is the quirky shops in the side streets which give this area its appeal. Locally made goods are available in most of the shops mentioned below. When you feel like a break from shopping, Café Cristal (Calle Pedromo 3) offers freshly squeezed fruit juices at outdoor tables. There are also several pavement cafes along Calle Mayor, with nearby buskers.

Hats

Ezquerra (Calle Travieso 4) is one of a kind, an old-fashioned hat shop selling sombreros and *cachorros canarios* (the black felt hats worn by Canarian men) as well as *mantillas* and Canarian desert boots.

Books

A few doors away from Ezquerra, **La Librería del Cabildo Insular** (Calle Cano 24) is a bookshop run by the Gran Canarian government, with a wide range of books on Gran Canaria as well as walking maps and Canarian music on CD.

Crafts

Also worth seeking out is **Fedac** (Calle Domingo J Navarro 7) a government-sponsored craft shop which sells goods direct from the producers at reasonable, non-profit prices. Among the items are pottery, basketware, lace, bone-handled knives, jewellery, musical instruments and mini Canarian balconies.

Atarecos (Calle Peregrina 4), hidden away in a quiet back street, features local handicrafts as well as Latin American clothing and jewellery. This narrow street of traditional balconied houses also contains several antiques shops.

On Calle Mayor itself, **Natura Selection** is a branch of a well-known chain, at No 67, offering fairly traded goods (silk, cotton, candles, crafts) from around the world, together with New Age books and music.

Confectionery

Casa Ricardo (corner of Calle Mayor and Calle Losero) is the confectionery shop of your dreams, with a colourful pick-and-mix selection of strawberry golf balls, orange bonbons, heart-shaped lollipops and peach-flavoured liquorice.

MARKETS

Mercado de Vegueta (▶ 66): this is Las Palmas' oldest and best food market.

Mercado Central (Calle Galicia): this second food market is situated conveniently close to Avenida Mesa y López.

Mercado del Puerto (Calle Albareda): a covered market down by the port, with more of an international flavour. Seafood and fresh produce are sold inside, and stalls around the edge cater for foreign sailors passing through.

Mercado de las Flores (Plaza de Santo Domingo): arts, crafts and flower market which takes place on Sunday mornings in this attractive old town square.

Rastro (Parque Santa Catalina): lively flea-market on Sunday mornings, featuring everything from second-hand books and videos to old clothes, plants and a few genuine antiques.

PUEBLO CANARIO

This Canarian-style "village" of traditional architecture (▶ 68) contains several souvenirs and craft shops where you can buy T-shirts, folk costumes, ceramics, books and collections of Gran Canarian folk music. The traditional folk music accompanies the traditional folk-dancing, which you can see in regular performances on Thursday and Monday.

Where to...
Be Entertained

MUSIC AND DRAMA

Theatre and concert listings can be found in the daily newspapers *Canarias 7*, *La Provincia* and *Diario de Las Palmas*. There are also various English-language newspapers such as the *Island Sun*, available from the kiosks in Parque Santa Catalina and aimed firmly at an expatriate readership. If you have internet access, it is worth consulting the daily programme of cultural events on www.canarynet.com, which you can find by clicking on 'agenda' in the left-hand column.

Plays are staged at the **Teatro Pérez Galdós**, designed by Miguel Martín Fernández de la Torre with murals by his brother Néstor. A favourite haunt of the Las Palmas bourgeoisie, this was home to the Las Palmas Philharmonic Society and the annual opera festival until the opening of the **Auditorio Alfredo Kraus** (▶ 70). The theatre is currently undergoing major restoration work and is expected to reopen in 2003.

The other principal theatres are **Teatro Guiniguada**, on the opposite side of the road which separates Triana from Vegueta, and the **Teatro Cuyás**, which opened in 2000 in a former cinema in Triana. Look out too for performances at a pair of cultural centres in Triana, the CIC (Centro Insular de Cultura) and CICCA (Centro de Iniciativas de la Caja de Canarias).

Since its opening in 1997, the **Auditorio Alfredo Kraus** on Las Canteras beach has become the main concert venue in the city and the largest performance space in the Canary Islands. The symphony hall holds more than 1,600 people, with a window behind the stage giving spectacular ocean views. In addition to opera and classical music, the auditorium is used for concerts ranging from salsa to Latin jazz.

It is also the principal venue for several major **festivals**, including an international film festival (Jan/Feb), dance festival (Feb/Mar), opera festival (Apr/May), and festival of Spanish light opera (Oct/Nov). The area facing the auditorium is being developed as an open-air concert space, Parque de la Música.

The **WOMAD** (World of Music, Arts and Dance) festival takes place each November in Parque Santa Catalina, with free events featuring musicians from around the world. For something closer to home, there is Canarian folk music and dancing twice a week at the Pueblo Canario (▶ 68).

FILMS

The latest international blockbusters dubbed into Spanish, as well as contemporary Spanish films, are shown at multiplex cinemas around the city. The biggest are in the Las Arenas and La Ballena shopping centres, though the Royal and Monopol cinemas are convenient options in the centre of town. Full listings can be found in the local newspapers. An international film festival takes place (Oct/Nov) in venues including the Teatro Pérez Galdós and Auditorio Alfredo Kraus (▶ 70).

NIGHTLIFE

As in the rest of Spain, nightlife starts late and few people would consider going out before 10 pm. The "in" places come and go, but as a general rule the old town districts of Vegueta and Triana have a more sophisticated appeal, while the focus of young nightlife is around **Parque Santa Catalina** and the port. The exception is the area around Plaza de Cairasco, which is heaving every evening as students gather outside the terrace bars of Alameda Café, Old Stone's and the Hotel Madrid(▶72). Around the corner, La Floridita is a re-creation of a famous Havana cocktail bar, while Taberna de las Ranas is a popular night-time haunt on the edge of the Boulevard Monopol shopping centre.

As the night wears on, *la movida* (the scene) shifts downtown. The bars on the north side of Plaza de España are lively around midnight, and there is plenty of action on the *terrazas* (terrace bars) around Parque Santa Catalina. The area between Parque Santa Catalina and the port is where you will encounter the seamier side of Las Palmas, and it is wise not to wander alone in this area at night. Most bars shut around 2 am, but the discos stay open for a few hours after that.

For those who enjoy a flutter, the **Casino Las Palmas** (open daily from 4 pm to 4 am) is inside the Hotel Santa Catalina. Blackjack, baccarat and roulette are all played here. Men are expected to wear a tie, and a passport is also required.

FESTIVALS

Día de los Reyes (5 Jan): the eve of Epiphany offers a street parade for the city's children, led by characters playing the Three Wise Men.

Carnival (Feb): the pre-Lenten Carnival celebrations in Las Palmas are the biggest on the island, beginning with the election of the Carnival Queen and continuing with open-air street parties, masked balls and fancy-dress parades.

Corpus Christi (late May/early Jun): the streets of the old town are decorated with flowers and Plaza de Santa Ana a carpet of floral displays.

San Juan (24 Jun): pagan and Christian rituals and a celebration of the founding of Las Palmas. Bonfires are lit on the beaches on the night of 24 Jun, the high point of a week of concerts, theatre, dance and sporting activities.

La Virgen del Carmen (16 Jul): processions of fishing boats in La Isleta and Puerto de la Luz in honour of the Virgin, patron saint of fishermen.

Fiestas de la Naval (6 Oct): La Isleta celebrates the victory of the Spanish Armada over the British explorer Sir Francis Drake in 1595.

OUTDOOR ACTIVITIES

Sailing, windsurfing and **scuba-diving** courses are available at the Muelle Deportivo marina and the Real Club Victoria at the eastern end of Playa de las Canteras. The best place for ordinary surfing is at the western end of Las Canteras, beneath the Auditorio Alfredo Kraus (▶70).

UD Las Palmas football team play host to top Spanish teams Valencia, Barcelona and Real Madrid. Most matches are on Sunday afternoons September to June at the **Estadio Insular** (Calle Pío XII 29; tel: 928 241342; Bus Nos 2, 3, 20, 22, 25, 81). Tickets for most games are sold on the day.

One sport which is peculiar to Las Palmas is **Vela Latina**, regattas featuring small "lateen" boats with outsize sails and a crew of between eight and 12.

Regattas take place most weekends between April and October, on Saturday afternoons and Sunday mornings, to take advantage of the prevailing trade winds. The boats race along the east coast of Las Palmas from Playa de la Laja to Playa de Alcaravaneras.

The best vantage points are the Muelle Deportivo marina, or anywhere along the Avenida Marítima promenade.

The North

Getting Your Bearings

For many people, the north is the true essence of Gran Canaria. Las Palmas may be more exciting, the central mountains more dramatic, and the south more sunshine, but the real Gran Canaria is found in the fertile hills and valleys of the north. This is where the Guanche kingdoms established their capitals, at Telde and Gáldar. And, apart from Las Palmas, this is still where the majority of Canarios live, in towns like Arucas and Agaete, Gáldar and Guía, Telde and Teror, where tourism is important but where there is still more than one way of making a living.

The north is not without tourist ambitions, but the clouds which produce its famously green landscape are the same ones that keep most tourists away. When the trade winds reach Gran Canaria, they bring with them a thick bank of cloud that hovers over the north of the island and fills the air with moisture.

★ Don't Miss

At Your Leisure

Page 77: Gran Canaria's
north coastline with Las
Palmas in the distance

Above: Telde

Left: The view along
the northwest coast

Rain is not
uncommon here,
and sometimes
the sun is hardly
seen for days at a time.
Agriculture thrives, from the
banana belts around Arucas and Gáldar (though these days the banana industry
is in serious decline) to the plains of San Mateo and the tropical valley of Agaete.
Most of the fruit and vegetables which you can buy in Gran Canaria are grown
in this area.

It is not just farming and fishing which have survived. Many of Gran Canaria's
indigenous crafts are still produced here, from the pottery workshops of La
Atalaya to the stonework of Arucas. This is also where you will encounter the
most authentic town and village fiestas, such as the annual pilgrimage to Teror
or the surviving pagan ritual of beating branches in the water in an effort to
bring rain at Puerto de las Nieves.

You cannot claim to know Gran Canaria until you have spent some time in
the north. There are some remarkable sights here, including a well-preserved
Guanche granary and the island's most spectacular crater, but what most people
remember are the small towns and villages, the markets and the volcanic hills
which give this region its special character.

This varied tour takes you from a botanical garden on the edge of Las Palmas to a fertile valley overlooking the northwest coast.

Northern Gran Canaria in Three Days

Day One

Morning
Spend the morning at the **Jardín Canario** (➤ 85), admiring its collection of native Canarian plants (right), then have a traditional Canarian lunch at the restaurant that overlooks the gardens.

Afternoon
A short drive leads to **Caldera de Bandama** (➤ 82), where you can walk off your lunch with a hike down into the crater or enjoy a round of golf at Spain's oldest golf club (below) before spending the night at the **Bandama Golf Hotel** (➤ 42).

Day Two

Morning
The road from Bandama to Santa Brígida passes through **La Atalaya** (➤ 83), where it is worth a brief stop to see the Guanche-style pottery, made at workshops throughout the village. At Santa Brígida, take the C811 into the mountains, climbing through pinewoods to **Vega de San Mateo** (➤ 96) where you turn right towards **Teror** (➤ 87). After a twisting drive you should arrive in this town in time to visit the basilica and museum before lunch at **El Secuestro** (➤ 100).

Afternoon

A minor road from Teror leads to
Arucas (➤ 96), where you can visit
the neo-Gothic "cathedral" (right) and
stroll through the streets and
gardens of the town. Spend the
night at **La Hacienda del Buen Suceso**
(➤ 41), a smart rural hotel at the
centre of a banana plantation.

Day Three

Morning

Drive down to the coast and take
the GC2 towards **Gáldar** (➤ 98).
When you reach the outskirts of
Santa Maria de Guía, double back
on the C801 (the old road to Las
Palmas) to visit the Guanche caves at **Cenobio de Valerón** (➤ 90).
Afterwards, stop in **Santa Maria de Guía** (➤ 97) to taste the
excellent local cheeses at Santiago Gil Romero's shop on the
high street. Return to the GC2 and drive down to **Puerto de las Nieves**
for a seafood lunch by the beach (➤ 100).

Afternoon

Take a walk around the harbour in Puerto de las Nieves, admiring the
fishing boats and the **Dedo de Díos rock** (➤ 93, below). From here you can
drive up the lush **Valle de Agaete** (➤ 93). If you feel like staying longer,
the **Princesa Guayarmina spa hotel** at the head of the valley (➤ 42)
offers peace, solitude, mountain walks and organic vegetables from
their own farm.

❷

Caldera de Bandama

This perfectly formed crater (*caldera*), 1km wide and 200m deep, has walls of volcanic rock and a fertile valley at its centre. Although it has been dormant for hundreds of years, the existence of a "hot spot" just below the surface suggests that the volcano may yet erupt again. There are fine views over the crater from the nearby peak, and a walk down onto the valley floor gives a close-up look at Gran Canaria's volcanic scenery – not to mention its most isolated house.

The crater takes its name from Daniel Van Damm, a 16th-century Dutch farmer who first planted vines here. Begin by heading up to the **Pico de Bandama** (574m) for the best overall view. A spiralling road leads up here from the village; from the bus stop it takes around 30 minutes to walk. The

Gran Canaria's *calderas* were formed millions of years ago

Take your time if you are walking down to the crater floor

views from the peak stretch as far as Las Palmas and occasionally to Fuerteventura. The bowl-shaped crater is spread out beneath you, while across the crater the lush green fairways of Spain's oldest golf club (Real Club de Golf de Las Palmas) form a dramatic contrast to the dark volcanic ash below.

The **walk** down into the crater is straightforward enough but you need to be prepared for a steep, tiring climb on the way back. Allow at least 90 minutes, more if you have a bus to catch. The path begins by the bus stop. Follow the lane which runs downhill past a small group of houses and into the crater. The path is cobbled at first, but soon becomes slippery and you need good shoes. If you don't want to go the whole way, about halfway down there is a *mirador* built onto a rocky platform with excellent views.

From here the path drops down sharply to the crater floor, alive with olive trees, cactus, borage and broom. Just after passing a large boulder on your right, turn right and then immediately left on to a narrow path which makes a complete circuit of the valley. At the centre of the crater is a half-abandoned farmhouse, incongruously numbered 44. Two huge eucalyptus trees offer shade, and an old wine press is hidden behind the shed. From the farmhouse, a path climbs back out of the crater. As you climb, look out for a group of **Guanche cave dwellings**, dramatically set into the crater walls.

La Atalaya

The road from Bandama to Santa Brígida passes through La Atalaya, a village of cave houses whose inhabitants are famous for their unglazed pottery. Everything here is made in the aboriginal style, hand-shaped out of volcanic clay without the use of a wheel and baked in woodburners rather than electric kilns. The pottery is sold from cave workshops close to the village square, where murals of local potters pay tribute to this ancient art.

The Real
Club de Golf
de Las Palmas
overlooks
the crater

TAKING A BREAK

The village bar, **Los Geranios**, beside the bus stop serves
excellent sandwiches and snacks, but you cannot always rely
on it being open. A **shop** at the summit of Pico de Bandama
sells ice-creams and cold drinks.

➕ 179 E4 ✉ 2km south of Tafira Alta, reached via C811 from Las Palmas
🚌 311, 312 from Las Palmas

CALDERA DE BANDAMA: INSIDE INFO

Top tips Take a **picnic** and **plenty of water** if you are walking down into the crater.
• It is a good idea to wear **long trousers** for this walk because of the sharp bushes
beside the narrow path.

In more depth It is possible to walk right **around the rim** of the caldera, with
views down into the crater from every angle. This walk is around 3km long and
takes 1½ hours.

   Start by taking the road from the village towards Pico de Bandama; after a
few minutes, as the road bends to the left, look out for a small parking area to
your right. From here a path leads to the ridge of the crater and continues around
the rim. It is narrow in places and quite vertiginous, but experienced walkers
will have no difficulty. After circling the crater, the path dips and then climbs to
the edge of the golf course, from where a short walk along the road leads back
to the village.

❹

Jardín Canario

Despite their small size, the Canary Islands harbour an extraordinary abundance of plant life, with many varieties of cactus and wildflowers growing only here. The islands are a refuge for more than 500 endemic plant species and many of them can be seen close up at Spain's largest botanical garden.

These gardens were laid out in 1952 on the steep slopes of the Guiniguada ravine. Most visitors arrive at the upper entrance (buses from Las Palmas stop here), where there is a *mirador* and a bust of the historian and naturalist Don José de Viera y Clavijo. From here you can look out over the entire gardens and the network of paths snaking down into the gorge.

You could easily spend an hour or two exploring at random, but it is best to head for the lower entrance and work your way back up to the top. Begin in **Plaza Matías Vega**, dominated by Canary palms. Near here, the **Jardín de las Islas** contains native species including the cardón, a cactus-like shrub which grows wild on the hillsides and is the botanical symbol of Gran Canaria.

Walk through the Jardín de las Islas to reach the **Jardín de Cactus**, a cactus garden with more than 2,000 varieties from across the world. Here you will find aloe vera and prickly pear, both prevalent on Gran Canaria. The path leads around the nursery to **Plaza Fernando Navarro**, where a small ornamental garden is devoted to the plants of Macronesia, the group of volcanic islands that includes the Canaries, Madeira and the Azores. Among the endemic species to be found here is the yellow-flowering Teror broom.

Cross the wooden bridge to return to the left bank and begin the climb out of the gorge. Passing through woods of Canary pine, you reach **Paseo de los Dragos**, a footpath

The cactus gardens include both native and imported species, such as these *echinocactus grusonii* from Mexico (below left)

Dragon trees were revered by the Guanches for their sacred and healing properties

lined with dragon trees. This distinctive tree, closely related to the yucca, is mostly found on Tenerife. Its bark can be scratched to produce a resin known as "dragon's blood" which was used by the original inhabitants of the Canary Islands as a medicine. The path climbs past a pair of twin dragon trees to return to the *mirador*.

TAKING A BREAK

The restaurant at the **upper entrance** to the gardens is known for its excellent Canarian cuisine.

🚹 179 E4 ✉ 7km from Las Palmas on C811 to Tafira Alta ✉ 928 353604 🕐 Daily 9–6 🚌 301, 302, 303, 305, 311, 312 💷 Free

---

JARDÍN CANARIO: INSIDE INFO

Top tips If you are **driving**, you can reach the lower entrance to the gardens by taking a right fork in Tafira Alta and following the minor road to Las Palmas. However, there is not much parking down here and you may be better off using the large **car-park** at the upper entrance.

● If you are coming by **bus**, the trip can be combined with the Caldera de Bandama (▶ 82), though you need to make an early start to give yourself enough time. **Six buses a day** connect Las Palmas with Bandama, stopping outside the Jardín Canario.

Hidden gem Look out for **La Fuente de los Sabios** (Fountain of the Wise), an unexpected man-made monument in a garden full of natural beauty. The fountain is dedicated to foreign naturalists who have worked in the Canaries – among them Sabin Barthelot and Philip Barker Webb, authors of the first natural history of the Canary Islands in 1835.

5

Teror

This charming town of cobbled streets, whitewashed houses and Spanish colonial architecture is also the centre of popular religion on Gran Canaria. Thoroughly restored and declared a historical monument in 1979, it is now a showpiece town where visitors come for a glimpse of Gran Canaria as it was.

Most people only stay for half an hour or so, which is a pity as Teror rewards a much longer visit. This is a place for ambling up and down side streets, or sitting in shady squares admiring the beautifully preserved stone mansions. Even a simple stroll along the main street, from the bus station to the basilica, turns into a voyage of discovery as your eyes are drawn constantly upwards by the details on the carved wooden balconies which adorn every façade.

The main street comes to an end at a large open square in front of the **Basílica de Nuestra Señora del Pino**. The Church of Our Lady of the Pine takes its name from an apparition of the Virgin rumoured to have appeared in a pine tree shortly after the Spanish Conquest of 1478. The statue of the Virgin dates from the 15th century and is revered across the island. Every year on 8 September, the anniversary of the original apparition, people make the pilgrimage from all over Gran

The main street in Teror is lined with fine old Canario houses

Catch a glimpse of the courtyard of the Manrique de Lara family home

Canaria for the island's biggest religious celebration. The Virgin of the Pine is not only the patron saint of Gran Canaria, such is her status that she has also been awarded the honorary rank of captain-general in the Spanish army.

The **basilica** itself is a neo-classical structure, completed in 1767 but incorporating an octagonal tower from an earlier church on this site. The three aisles are divided by tall stone columns which rise to a coffered wooden ceiling. Above the altar, the Virgin sits beneath a silver canopy in her finely embroidered robes. The emeralds which once adorned the statue were stolen in an audacious robbery in 1975.

The complex of historic buildings behind the basilica includes the former episcopal palace, now a library and exhibition centre. In the square in front of the church, the **Casa Museo de los Patrones de la Virgen del Pino** is one of the best surviving examples of a traditional Canarian town house. The house belongs to the Manrique de Lara family, custodians of the Virgin of the Pine, and has been in the same family since it was built in the 17th century.

The rooms, filled with family heirlooms, portraits and antique furniture, lead off from a central courtyard overlooked by a rickety wooden balcony. The stables contain a collection of carriages including the state coach

Ay Teror!

Ay Teror! is the title of a popular Canario folk song, with words by local historian Néstor Alamo (1906–94). The song can often be heard at festivals and is also featured on CDs by folklore groups such as Los Gofiones and Mestisay.

used by Alfonso XIII, and the garage has a classic 1951 Triumph Renown car imported from England by Don Agustín Manrique de Lara.

A tour of the house gives a fascinating insight into the lives of the Canarian nobility. Don Agustín, who was born in 1909, still lives in the house for one or two weeks each year during the fiesta of La Virgen del Pino (► 102).

TAKING A BREAK

There are several cafés on and around Plaza del Pino, but for a really good rustic meal you should head for **El Secuestro** (► 100), on a hill overlooking the town.

🟦 179 D4 🚌 216 from Las Palmas

Basilica
✉ Plaza del Pino 🕔 Daily 7–noon, 2–9 🎫 Free

Casa Museo de los Patrones de la Virgen del Pino
✉ Plaza del Pino 🕔 Mon–Thu and Sat 11–6.30, Sun 10–2.30 🎫 Inexpensive

TEROR: INSIDE INFO

Top tip Visit Teror on a **Sunday morning**, when the area around the basilica is taken over by a lively **market**, with stalls selling breads, cheeses and the local speciality, a soft pâté-like version of spicy chorizo sausage.

Hidden gem Don't miss **Plaza Teresa de Bolívar** (below), a small square just off Plaza del Pino, named after the first wife of the revolutionary Simon Bolívar. This peaceful square features intricately carved stone benches and a Gothic fountain at its centre, as well as a bust of Bolívar, who is best known for liberating the South American colonies from Spanish rule. Teresa de Bolívar, who grew up in Teror, was the daughter of a noble Canario family. She died of yellow fever less than a year after her marriage to Simon Bolívar in 1801.

❽

Cenobio de Valerón

This complex of honeycomb caves set into a natural arch in the rockface is not only the best-preserved but also the most accessible of all Gran Canaria's Guanche sites. Dating from before the time of the 15th-century Spanish invasion, these artificial caves are among the best examples of aboriginal rock-carving on the island.

The word *cenobio* means convent and it was once thought that this was a Guanche nunnery, housing *harimaguadas* (vestal virgins) and daughters of the nobility who were sent here in preparation for marriage and child-birth. Such places did exist, but these days archaeologists agree that the Cenobio de Valerón was in fact a grain store.

Some 300 **chambers** are carved into the rock, linked by a network of steps and passages. Such granaries were built in high places to protect them from attack, and volcanic rock was chosen as it was easily manoeuvred using

Summit Meetings
The summit above the caves, Montaña del Gallego, was a *tagoror*, a place of assembly where the Guanche council would meet with the *guanarteme* (king).

Right: The granary was protected from thieves by its hillside position

Below: The caves were originally built to store surplus grain after the harvest

tools made of stone and bones. This particular site was ideal. The natural overhang of the rock provided shelter from the rain, while its east-facing position ensured plentiful sun.

The caves are now open to the elements, but at one time they would have been covered by wooden doors in order to preserve the grain. Recent studies suggest that the various silos belonged to different families, identified by *pintaderas* (terracotta seals), whose designs were painted onto the walls. If this is true, it would indicate a high degree of social organisation among the pre-Hispanic people of Gran Canaria.

Access to the caves is by a steep staircase built into the rock. For reasons of safety and conservation, it is essential to stick to the path. Entry into the caves themselves is strictly forbidden.

🞡 178 C5 ✉ 3km east of Guía on C801, the old road to Las Palmas ☎ 928 381368 🕘 Wed–Sun 10–5 🚌 102, 103 from Las Palmas 💶 Free

CENOBIO DE VALERÓN: INSIDE INFO

Top tip Although admission to the caves is **free**, the guard at the entrance gate is always happy to accept a small tip.

▣

Valle de Agaete

Arriving in Valle de Agaete from one of the south coast resorts feels like stepping onto another planet. This bucolic valley, with its startling array of colours and unique subtropical climate, forms such a contrast to the arid landscapes of the south that you have to pinch yourself to remember that you are still in Gran Canaria.

Until recently the northwest coast was considered remote, but a new motorway and fast ferry service have turned this area into a stepping-stone between Las Palmas and Tenerife. Development has inevitably followed, especially by the port, though the old town of Agaete has retained much of its charm.

The town of **Agaete** was founded in 1481; a plaque near the church records the greetings of King Juan Carlos on its 500th anniversary, recalling his visit to "this pretty corner of Spain". It is a peaceful and attractive spot, with whitewashed houses and wooden balconies overflowing with plants. Locals sit around outside the 19th-century church in the shade of Plaza de la Constitución, or stroll in the Huerto de las Flores, a botanical garden where Tomás Morales (➤ 97) found inspiration.

The 7km **Valle de Agaete** climbs gently from Agaete towards the pinewoods of the Tamadaba massif. This is a place of almost mythical beauty, scented with honeysuckle, jasmine, bougainvillea, geraniums and Canarian pine. The fertile slopes support mangoes, papaya, oranges, lemons, grapefruit,

Agaete produces much of Gran Canaria's fruit crop

Fishing boats are washed up on the beach at Puerto de las Nieves

The Ermita de la Virgen de las Nieves

avocados and figs. The road ends at **Los Berrazales**, where there is a spa hotel and a footpath leading to the high sierra. There are breathtaking views over the valley and out to sea.

Back in Agaete, an arched bridge leads across the mouth of the barranco to **Puerto de las Nieves**. This one-time fishing port is said to have taken its name from the snow (*nieve*) which is often visible on Mount Teide on Tenerife. A small chapel, **Ermita de la Virgen de las Nieves**, is dedicated to the Virgin of the Snows, patron of local fishermen. Models of fishing boats hang from the wooden rafters, but the real treasure is a 16th-century Flemish triptych of the Virgin and Child by Joos Van Cleve. Only the central panel usually hangs here; the side panels, featuring St Antony and St Francis, are in the parish church at Agaete. The chapel is usually kept locked, though it is open for Mass on Saturday evenings and Sunday mornings.

Quiet during the week, Puerto de las Nieves gets crowded with visitors from Las Palmas at weekends. There is a pebble beach in the inner harbour, for swimming and snorkelling, and seafood restaurants on the promenade. Six ferries a day leave for Tenerife, an hour away by boat. From the harbour end of the beach you can look out over **Dedo de Dios** (Finger of God), a slender basalt pillar left behind by erosion and said to resemble a finger pointing to the heavens. It is silhouetted against the base of the cliffs at the start of the **Andén Verde** route.

A new hotel in Puerto de las Nieves has been built close to an old Guanche cemetery. All that remains is a model of what the cemetery might have looked like. Among the finds was an 8th-century coffin, now in the Museo Canario in Las Palmas (▶ 56).

Andén Verde

The most spectacular coastal drive on Gran Canaria reaches its climax at the so-called Andén Verde (green platform), just north of San Nicolás de Tolentino. The best viewpoint is from the Mirador del Balcón, where there is space to pull off the road and walk down to the viewing platform beneath the car-park. From here you look out along a rocky coastline to the headland of Punta Góngora. Bring some binoculars and you may be able to see dolphins basking out at sea. This drive can be incorporated into a complete circuit of the island (▶ 164).

TAKING A BREAK

Casa Romántica (▶ 100) is a popular restaurant with its own
tropical gardens where bananas, citrus fruit and avocados are
grown. Canaries sing and parrots squawk as you stroll around
the grounds. If you don't want a full meal, go to the bar for a
glass of fresh papaya juice or a cup of coffee from beans grown
on the estate.

The Dedo de
Díos (Finger of
God) provides
a dramatic
local landmark

🖽 178 C4 🚌 101 from Las Palmas to Agaete; 102 from Las Palmas to Valle
de Agaete; 103 from Las Palmas to Puerto de las Nieves

VALLE DE AGAETE: INSIDE INFO

Top tip Agaete and Puerto de las Nieves are the setting for one of Gran Canaria's
oldest festivals, **Bajada de la Rama** (▶ 102), which takes place in August.

In more depth From the top of the valley there are **walks** into the mountains
and the Tamadaba pinewoods. One popular excursion is to take the well-marked
track which starts above the Princess Guayarmina Hotel and leads in around an
hour to the hilltop hamlets of El Sao and El Hornillo.

At Your Leisure

❶ Telde

Gran Canaria's second town is almost totally off the tourist trail, yet it is easy to reach and has a very attractive and well-restored old quarter.

The most appealing area (*barrio*) is San Juan, reached by following the signposts from the large roundabout near the bus station. This was the site of the original Spanish settlement and it contains a number of old Canario houses built in distinctive Mudéjar (Moorish-Gothic) style soon after the Spanish Conquest in 1478. The district is centred around a charming main square, Plaza San Juan, where the church of San Juan Bautista (open from 5pm daily) features an ornate Flemish altarpiece and a revered statue of Christ, sculpted out of maize by Mexican Indians in the 16th century. Behind the church, a small park contains a children's playground, caged birds and a miniature zoo.

Opposite the plaza, a narrow lane leads across an aqueduct past citrus trees to another historic *barrio*, San Francisco, with whitewashed houses, cobbled streets and an 18th-century church. The two districts are joined by Calle León y Castillo, named after the brothers Fernando (1842–1918) and Juan León y Castillo (1834–1912), the former a diplomat and politician, the latter the engineer responsible for Maspalomas lighthouse and Puerto de la Luz in Las Palmas. Their **family home** has been turned into a museum, with galleries displaying medals, decorations and 19th-century paintings. If you want to relax, Parque San Juan has footpaths and cycle trails, an open-air auditorium, botanical gardens and a lake.

➕ 179 E3 ✉ Tourist information office, Calle León y Castillo 2 ☎ 928 681336 🚌 12 from Las Palmas, 36 and 90 from Maspalomas

Fernando León y Castillo – Telde's favourite son

Casa Museo León y Castillo
✉ Calle León y Castillo 43 ☎ 928 691377 🕐 Mon–Fri 9–1 🎟 Free

Cuatro Puertas
Telde was the capital of one of the two Guanche kingdoms on Gran Canaria and there are several archaeological sites around the town. The most important is Cuatro Puertas, 4km out of Telde on the road to Ingenio, where four separate entrances lead to a cave chamber where sacred rituals and fertility rites are believed to have been held.

🄈 Vega de San Mateo

This prosperous agricultural town at the foot of the sierra is best known for its weekly market, which begins on Saturday and reaches a climax on Sunday morning. Most of the action takes place in a large hangar on the edge of town, with stalls devoted to fruit, vegetables, olives, bread, eggs, cheeses and wine, as well as fresh flowers and dried herbs for both culinary and medicinal use. There is also an open-air market featuring local crafts such as pottery and basketwork.

🞧 179 D4 🚌 303

🄇 Arucas

This former banana town, now more or less a satellite of Las Palmas, is dominated by the extraordinary cathedral-like church of San Juan Bautista. Designed by the Catalan architect Manuel Vega March in neo-Gothic, Modernist style, it was built between 1909 and 1977 out of the local blue-grey stone. Although the church is modern, it contains a number of old works of art, including a Virgin and Child by Cristóbal Hernández de Quintana (1659–1725). By the altar is a beautiful sculpture of Christ, carved in wood in 1940 by local artist Manolo Ramos González.

The streets around the church contain several more buildings in the same volcanic stone, known as *piedra de Arucas* or *piedra azul* (blue stone). Most of them date from the late 19th

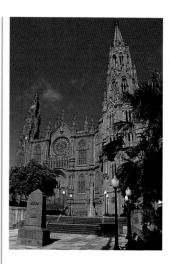

Arucas was built in the local volcanic stone

or early 20th centuries. Look out for the Heredad de Aguas (the water consortium), a splendid neo-classical building opposite the gardens.

Arucas is the centre of rum production on Gran Canaria and on a tour of the **Arehucas distillery** you can see barrels signed by King Juan Carlos, Julio Iglesias, Tom Jones and Montserrat Caballé. Included are free tasting of rum and liqueurs.

Before you leave Arucas, drive up to the summit of **La Montaña**, the volcanic cone overlooking the town. The views stretch to Las Palmas and down to the north coast, with banana plantations visible all around. Bananas are still an important crop, but competition from Africa and Central America means that the industry is in decline and these days much of the fruit is left to rot on the trees.

🞧 179 D5 ✉ Tourist information office, Plaza de la Constitución 1
☎ 928 605815 🕐 Church: Daily 9.30–12.30, 4.30–7 🚌 210, 216 from Las Palmas

Arehucas distillery

🞧 179 D5 ✉ Era de San Pedro 2 (2km on the road to Gáldar) ☎ 928 624900
🕐 Mon–Fri 10–1 🎫 Free

For Kids

Reptilandia (tel: 928 551269; open daily 11–5.30; moderate) is a small zoo run by British naturalists Jim and Chris Pether on a hillside between Gáldar and Agaete. It is signposted from the Hoya de Pineda exit on the GC2. More than 150 species of reptiles are kept here, including snakes, crocodiles and frogs, as well as parrots, monkeys and lemurs. Among the star attractions are a 7m Chinese python and a Komodo dragon, the world's largest species of lizard which can reach 100kg in weight.

117 from Las Palmas; 118, 123 from Arucas 🏛 Free

🟨7 Casa Museo Tomás Morales

The poet Tomás Morales (1884–1921) is known for his lyrical descriptions of his Gran Canarian homeland, and his birthplace in Moya has been turned into a museum.

The charming old house has a peaceful garden and rooms full of antique furniture and first editions of Morales' books. There are examples of his poetry all over the walls. Across the street, the parish church is precariously perched on the edge of a ravine, where two earlier churches fell into the gorge.

➕ 179 D5 ✉ Plaza de Tomás Morales, Moya ☎ 928 620217 ⏰ Mon–Fri 9–2, 4–8; Sat 10–2, 5–8; Sun 10–2 🚌 116,

🟨9 Santa Maria de Guía

Steep cobbled streets fan out from a leafy main square in one of the oldest towns on Gran Canaria, founded in 1483 when the conquistador Pedro de Vera distributed land among his soldiers and local noblemen.

The religious artist and sculptor Luján Pérez (1756–1815), whose works crop up all over Gran Canaria, was born here. It was Pérez who designed the neo-classical façade of the church of Santa María and there are several of his statues inside the church. The clock on the church tower was a gift from Pérez to the people of Guia.

However, the main reason for visiting Guía is to see Santiago Gil Moreno, whose wonderfully old-fashioned cheese shop is the best place to buy *queso de flor* (► 18).

➕ 178 C5 🚌 102, 103, 105 from Las Palmas

Firgas

The smallest town in Gran Canaria is famous for its mineral water. At the heart of the town is the much-photographed Paseo de Gran Canaria, a long flight of steps with a waterfall at the centre and a series of brightly coloured ceramic benches to one side (below). Each of the benches is devoted to one of the island's 21 municipalities, with a coat of arms and paintings of local scenes. Further up, Paseo de Canarias does the same thing for the seven Canary Islands. To get there, take bus Nos 201, 202, 203 or 220 from Las Palmas, or 207, 211 from Arucas.

⑩ Gáldar

Gáldar was one of the two capitals of the Guanches on Gran Canaria and the town makes much of its historic role as the court of the *guanartemes* (Guanche kings).

Street names recall the town's pre-Hispanic past, and a statue in the town centre, unveiled by King Juan Carlos in 1986, pays homage to Tenesor Semidan, the last king of Gáldar, who converted his people to Christianity and was baptised by the Spanish invaders.

Gáldar has plans to be a big tourist destination, but for now it is a busy town whose major attraction, the Cueva Pintada (Painted Cave), seems to be permanently closed for repairs. A reproduction of the cave can be seen in the Museo Canario in Las Palmas (➤ 56).

The most appealing part of the town is around Plaza de Santiago, a quiet square shaded by laurel trees in the shadow of a neo-classical church, built on the site of the palace of the Guanche kings.

Don't miss the enormous dragon tree in the courtyard of the town hall, which was planted in 1718.

✚ 178 B5　🚌 102, 103, 105 from Las Palmas

⑫ Sardina

Brightly painted fishing boats bob in the harbour at this cheerful fishing port, situated in the far northwest corner of the island. During pre-Hispanic times this may have been a significant port, and there are still several cave dwellings, now used as boathouses and seafood restaurants. You could try Terraza del Ancla for reasonably priced fresh sardines (➤ 101).

There are two small dark-sand beaches, and you can swim off the rocks with views across the harbour to the wild west coast. More popular with locals than with tourists, this is a good place for a relaxing afternoon by the sea.

✚ 178 B5　🚌 102, 103, 105 from Las PalmaS

The town of Gáldar can be clearly seen from the Hoya de Pineda. Gáldar was once a Guanche capital

Three Good Markets
- Arucas (Sat)
- Teror (Sun)
- Vega de San Mateo (Sun)

Sardina is still a working fishing port, with colourful fishing boats plying their trade

Y He Recordado

Y he recordado
El breve rincón de un pueblecillo
Una casa tranquila inundada de sol
Unas tapias musgosas de encarnado
ladrillo
Y un jardín que tenía limoneros en
flor.
And I remember
A small corner of a little village
A peaceful house flooded with
sunlight
Moss-covered walls of red brick
And a garden with lemon trees in
flower.

Tomás Morales
Las Rosas de Hércules (1922)

Where to...
Eat and Drink

Prices
Expect to pay per person for a meal, excluding drinks and service
£ under 12 Euros £ 12–24 Euros £ over 24 Euros

Most restaurants on Gran Canaria are open throughout the year, though they may close for an annual holiday, usually in August.

TEROR

El Secuestro ££
This rustic grillhouse on a hill overlooking Teror is totally devoted to meat. Carnivores will have a field day here, but vegetarians should definitely stay away. Pork chops, T-bone steaks, chorizo (spicy pork sausage) and morcilla (black pudding) are barbecued over an open fire, then served with watercress, roast potatoes and grilled tomato. Wooden tables and benches, and farming tools on the walls, complete the rustic approach. The easiest way to find the restaurant is by looking for the flags near the junction of the Valleseco and Arucas roads. You really need a car to get here.

➕ 179 D4 ⊠ Avenida Cabildo Insular 26 ☎ 928 630231
🕒 Tue–Fri noon–4.30, 7.30–midnight; Sat noon–midnight; Sun noon–5

VALLE DE AGAETE

Casa Romántica ££
Halfway up the Valle de Agaete, this restaurant is much frequented by tour groups who stroll in its gardens admiring the astonishing range of fruit trees and tropical plants. Although it mostly serves standard international cuisine, the restaurant also makes full use of the produce of its gardens, notably in the tropical fruit sorbets.

Another speciality is coffee, from the only coffee beans to grow in Gran Canaria. A shop sells packs of coffee for visitors to take home, as well as local produce such as aloe vera and papaya jam.

➕ 178 C4 ⊠ Valle de Agaete ☎ 928 898084 🕒 Daily 10–5.30

PUERTO DE LAS NIEVES

Las Nasas ££
The best of Canarian fish cooking is served at this simple beachside restaurant. The nautical theme dominates inside, with fishing nets, model boats and blue-and-white check tablecloths, or you can eat out of doors on the terrace just a few steps from the beach, watching the sunbathers, fishing boats and ferries leaving for Tenerife. Metal trays of red and green mojo sauce are brought by friendly waiters to your table, and the waiter will also recommend the fresh fish of the day, which you can have fried or grilled – though there are plenty of more elaborate seafood choices as well.

➕ 178 B5 ⊠ Calle Nuestra Señora de las Nieves 6 ☎ 928 898650
🕒 Daily noon–8

VEGA DE SAN MATEO

La Cantonera ££
This busy restaurant in a converted farmhouse specialises in Canarian country cooking. The adjoining cottages have been turned into a museum of rural life (open Mon–Sat 10–1) and the restaurant continues

the same theme, with antique farm implements on the walls and a huge bellows by the fire. The menu has classic dishes such as watercress soup and *cherne* (Atlantic grouper) in coriander sauce. Get here early to visit the museum and you can also have a tasting of local wines. There are also 15 rooms.

🏠 179 D4 ☒ Avenida de Tinamar ☎ 928 331374 ⏰ Mon–Sat 1–4, 8.30–midnight

ARUCAS

Meson de la Montaña ££

This restaurant on the top of the volcano overlooking Arucas has a strong element of kitsch. Service is formal, with waiters in waistcoats and bow ties, and the menu has Canarian and regional Spanish specialities as well as unusual dishes like beef in mango sauce. The extensive wine cellar includes Canarian wines. The food is very acceptable, but the main reason for coming here is the view, which takes in Las Palmas, the banana plantations and sometimes Tenerife. There is also a children's playground.

🏠 179 D5 ☒ Montaña de Arucas ☎ 928 601475 ⏰ Daily noon–midnight

SARDINA

Terraza del Ancla ££

This fish restaurant on the promenade captures the atmosphere of the *chiringuitos*, those beach huts which used to be in all of Spain's fishing ports serving fried sardines caught freshly that day. You eat at plastic tables on the pavement, but the views and the colourful fishing boats make up for any discomfort. Ask the waiter for the fresh catch of the day, which comes grilled, with toasted garlic and herbs. Paella and *sancocho* (Canarian fish stew) are served at weekends. An experience to be thoroughly recommended – simple but delicious.

🏠 178 B5 ☒ Avenida Antonio Rosas ☎ 928 551496 ⏰ Daily noon–2 am

Where to...
Shop

The weekly markets at Arucas (Sat), Teror (Sun) and Vega de San Mateo (Sun) have a good range of local produce, and there are daily covered markets at Arucas and Gáldar. The best place to buy pottery is in the cave village of La Atalaya (▶ 83).

ARUCAS

The Arehucas distillery shop (▶ 96) sells a range of light and dark rums, some of them aged for up to 12 years, along with rum-based liqueurs tasting of banana, orange, coffee, almonds and honey. A small shop in Plaza San Juan, in front of the church, sells Guanche-style pottery and artefacts fashioned out of volcanic stone.

SANTA MARÍA DE GUÍA

Guía is famous for its *queso de flor* (literally "flower cheese"), made in the highlands from a mixture of cow's and sheep's milk and curdled with thistle flowers.

The best place to buy it is from Santiago Gil Romero (Calle Marqués del Muni 34), on the main road running through the centre of town. Señor Romero loves his cheese and will share his love with anyone, proffering slices of mature *queso* and insisting that you wash it down with a glass of the local red wine. Cheeses mature on bamboo mats, the dusty shelves are piled high with wine bottles, and faded newspaper cuttings and football posters adorn the walls of this atmospheric shop.

Where to...
Be Entertained

FESTIVALS

San Juan Bautista (24 Jun): bonfires, dancing and cattle markets in Arucas and Telde in honour of their patron saint.

Santiago (25 Jul): traditional dancing and Canarian wrestling for the feast of St James in Gáldar.

Bajada de La Rama (4 Aug): locals from Agaete collect pine branches from the mountains and carry them down to the sea, where they thrash the waves with them to pray for rain. This is one of the oldest festivals in Gran Canaria, with rituals dating back to pre-Hispanic times.

Traída del Agua (12 Aug): locals shower visitors with water in the district of Lomo Magullo in Telde, in imitation of an ancient Guanche ritual whereby thanks were offered to Alcorán, the god of rain.

Santa María de Guía (15 Aug): traditional celebrations in Guía in honour of the patron saint.

La Virgen del Pino (8 Sep): pilgrims converge on Teror from all over Gran Canaria, bringing carts laden with fresh produce to lay at the feet of the Virgin in Gran Canaria's biggest popular religious festival.

Bajada del Cristo (Sep): the maize sculpture of Christ is taken down from the church in Telde and carried in procession through the town.

San Mateo (21 Sep): pilgrimage and street parties in Vega de San Mateo in honour of the patron saint.

Fiesta de la Manzana (first Sun in Oct): apple festival to celebrate the harvest in Valleseco, near Teror.

OUTDOOR ACTIVITIES

Golf

There are two golf courses in this region. A handicap certificate is advisable if you are thinking of visiting either of them. **Real Club de Golf de Las Palmas** (tel: 928 350104) is the oldest golf club in Spain, founded in 1891 and situated on the edge of the Caldera de Banadama (▶ 82). The undulating course has narrow fairways and facilities include a driving range and a floodlit putting green as well as a golf hotel. Visitors are welcome but you should try to avoid weekends. A second course has recently opened at **El Cortijo** near Telde (tel: 928 711111), 6km south of Las Palmas on the GC1 motorway. El Cortijo also features an 18-hole pitch-and-putt course which is illuminated at night.

Horse-riding

Riding lessons and organised outings are available at the Bandama Golf Club Riding School (tel: 928 351290).

Surfing

The waves along the **north coast** make for good surfing with body-boards. Some of the best spots are the beaches of Bañaderos, Quintanilla and San Andrés near Arucas, San Felipe near Guía and Bocabarranco near Gáldar.

Surfing equipment and body-boards can be hired at all of these beaches.

Spectator sports

The **Carrera de Campeones** is an international rally-driving championship which takes place on the Islas Canarias circuit near Telde in early December. Advance tickets are available from El Corte Inglés department store in Las Palmas. Tickets can also be bought at the entrance.

Central Mountains

Getting Your Bearings

Wild, windswept, majestic, magnificent, the centre of Gran Canaria is unique on the island. The mountains and valleys which make up the *cumbre* (central sierra) are the result of volcanic activity which began around 14 million years ago. Erosion has produced a stark, dramatic landscape of craters, gullies, canyons, cliffs and vast pillars of rock. Each new bend in the road reveals more startling views. The philosopher Miguel de Unamuno (1864–1937) called this area a "tempest of stone"; for the 17th-century historian Marín y Cubas, it was "a red ochre-coloured landscape like baked soil".

Two instantly identifiable landmarks stand guard over the sky-line, following you around wherever you go. One is the vast bulk of Roque Bentaiga, a sacred place in earlier times and now the centre of an archaeological park. The other is Roque Nublo, tall and slender, whose familiar silhouette has become a symbol of Gran Canaria.

Yet despite the grandeur of these impressive natural monuments, the mountains also have their softer side. There are

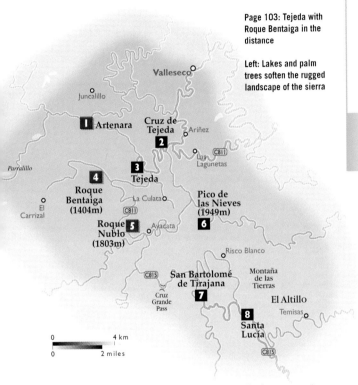

Page 103: Tejeda with
Roque Bentaiga in the
distance

Left: Lakes and palm
trees soften the rugged
landscape of the sierra

villages of white houses surrounded by almond groves and palm trees, and in
springtime the hillsides become a festival of colour, painted with wildflowers
such as cistus, lavender and broom. The dense pinewoods which once covered
these slopes may have disappeared, but the last remaining forest of Canary pines
at Tamadaba is a reminder of what might have been.

　There are two ways of exploring this region. Most people visit the mountains
on a day trip from the coast, dashing through in a hire car and admiring the
scenery through their windscreen. If this is all you have time for, do it – it will
be one of the highlights of your trip. Alternatively, if you can, stay the night, get
out in the mountains, breathe the air, smell the wild herbs, hike along the old
mule paths and ancient pilgrim routes which are being carefully restored, and
you will experience a side of Gran Canaria that few visitors ever see.

Breathtaking mountain scenery and a climb to the top of the island are the highlights of these two round trips from Cruz de Tejeda.

Central Gran Canaria in Two Days

Day One

Morning

Spend the morning in **Artenara** (➤ 108), Gran Canaria's highest town, enjoying views across the sierra. Climb up to the cave chapel above the town before lunch in the cave restaurant **La Silla** (right, ➤ 119).

Afternoon

Walk off lunch with a stroll in the Tamadaba pine woods (below). From the car-park and picnic area, a wide track leads through the woods to a series of reservoirs. Complete the circuit of the woods by car, enjoying the views of Tenerife across the water. Return through Artenara and **Tejeda** (➤ 116) to **Cruz de Tejeda** (➤ 115), where you can stay the night at **El Refugio** (➤ 43). Alternatively, confident

drivers can make a spectacular round trip through **Acusa** and
El Carrizal (➤ 117) on a scary, twisting and turning road which begins
around 3km east of Tamadaba. Although the distances are not great,
you would probably need the whole afternoon for this trip.

Evening
Climb the hill behind **El Refugio** after a good meal to watch the sun set.

Day Two

Morning
Follow the snaking road downhill back towards Tejeda, with the two
monoliths of Roque Bentaiga and Roque Nublo looming large over the
landscape. After bypassing Tejeda, take the right turn to **Roque Bentaiga**
(above, ➤ 110), where you can visit the archaeological museum and climb
the short path towards the rock. Continue south to Ayacata for lunch at one
of the roadside bars. Viuda de Viera serves excellent salads as well as the
traditional *papas arrugadas* (Canarian potatoes).

Afternoon
Take the minor road from Ayacata to
Cruz de Tejeda. A stone cross
(right) marks the centre of Gran
Canaria at the top of the mountain
pass. The first stop is La Goleta car-
park, the start of the path to **Roque
Nublo** (➤ 112). After climbing to the summit,
continue on this road, passing almond groves and
campsites before reaching a crossroads. Turn right at
the crossroads for **Pico de las Nieves** (➤ 116),
Gran Canaria's highest peak. After taking in the
views, return along the same road, visiting the
interpretation centre at the Mirador de
Becerra on the way (➤ 115).

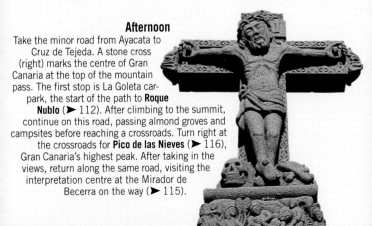

❶

Artenara

At an altitude of 1,260m, Artenara is the highest town on Gran Canaria, with unrivalled views over the central sierra and the pine-covered hills. It is also one of the oldest towns on the island, continuously inhabited since before the Spanish invasion of 1478. Artenara was the Guanche name for the town; it was changed by the Spanish conquerors to San Matías de Artenara, but has since reverted to its original name.

The earliest inhabitants carved **cave dwellings** out of the rock and many of these are still lived in today. Some of the caves have become second homes for the people of Las Palmas, and others are let out as holiday cottages. The best-known cave in Artenara is the sanctuary housing the **Virgen de la Cuevita** (Virgin of the Cave), the focus of one of the island's most spectacular festivals (► 120). The chapel is believed to have been built by 14th-century Mallorcan monks who visited Gran Canaria as missionaries before the Spanish Conquest and enlisted local converts to help.

To find the chapel, follow the signs to La Cuevita from the church square at the centre of town. Only the belfry on the roof suggests that there is anything special about this cave. The present **chapel** dates from the 17th century, with an altar, pulpit, choirstand and confessional hewn out of the red volcanic rock. Inside a niche sits the carved wooden statue of the Virgin, with the infant Christ in her arms.

The humility of this scene contrasts sharply with Artenara's other notable sight, a huge Rio de Janeiro-style **statue of Christ** with arms outstretched standing on a hilltop overlooking the town. It is worth climbing up here for the **views** of the *cumbre*. The two principal landmarks, Roque Bentaiga (► 110) and Roque Nublo (► 112), are clearly visible on the skyline and there is a vast panorama over the Tejeda valley and the surrounding cliffs. Beneath the statue of Christ, a tunnel leads through the mountain to the cave restaurant La Silla (► 119).

On the northern edge of Artenara, above the park, there is a *mirador* with a vista of the Tamadaba pinewoods. The **Pinar de Tamadaba** is the last surviving primeval forest on Gran Canaria and it is covered with Canary pines which grow to more than 30m high. A one-way circuit leads around the forest, where pine cones and needles are strewn across the road. There are many footpaths here, as well as a campsite and picnic area.

An enormous statue of Christ dominates the town

The view from Artenara

Cave houses are found side by side with modern buildings

The cave village of **Lugarejos**, near Tamadaba, is a centre of production for traditional pottery. All the raw materials are gathered locally – red ochre, clay, pine needles and cones, which fuel the kilns. The earthenware can be bought at an eco-museum and interpretation centre in Lugarejos.

TAKING A BREAK

La Silla (➤ 119) offers honest Canarian food and is worth a visit for the views alone.

🔲 178 C4 ✉ 220 from Las Palmas

ARTENARA: INSIDE INFO

Top tip Remember that it can get very **cold** up here in winter and even on summer evenings.

In more depth The flat-topped tableland at **Acusa**, near Artenara, was the site of a Guanche settlement and is one of only three places in Gran Canaria where mummies have been found. It is situated at the start of a spectacular drive, with narrow roads tumbling down to the Barranco de la Aldea and returning through the village of **El Carrizal** (➤ 117). The mummies, which were wrapped in cured goatskins and placed in woven rush bags, are on display in the **Museo Canario** in Las Palmas (➤ 56).

4

Roque Bentaiga

This 1,404m outcrop, left behind by volcanic eruptions more than three million years ago, was both a sacred area and a place of refuge for the Guanches. Recent excavations have uncovered several groups of cave houses, together with barns, cattle pens and burial sites. An *almogarén*, a place of ritual worship and sacrifice that the Guanches built in the highest and least accessible places on the island, was found here. Some of the caves are painted with fertility symbols, and this is also where the first discoveries of aboriginal writing using a version of the Libyan-Berber alphabet were made.

According to historical accounts, Roque Bentaiga was the site of a fierce **battle** in 1483 as the Spanish conquerors attempted to subdue the Canario natives. One of the conquerors, Sedeño, has described how the Canarios fled to Bentaiga following a defeat at Ajodar (La Aldea): "Short of provisions, the Canarios and their leader abandoned Ajodar at nightfall and started their climbing march along the San Nicolás valley on their way to another fortress known as Bentaiga, where they managed to obtain supplies. The stronghold is surrounded by cliffs at the top of which there are several caves with capacity for many people, although the paths leading up to them are dangerous."

It is easy to see how this isolated rock could provide a natural fortress. Chronicles of the conquest describe how the

Roque Bentaiga stands out above the mountain landscape

ROQUE BENTAIGA: INSIDE INFO

In more depth Cueva del Rey, 2km west of Roque Bentaiga, is one of the largest man-made caves in Gran Canaria, approximately 20m long and 11m wide. The name suggests that it was used by a Guanche king (*rey*), but it seems to have been divided into a series of smaller chambers, which may have been used as sanctuaries or meeting places. The entrance to the cave can be seen high in the cliff face near a hamlet of shepherds' houses. Some of the nearby caves are still in use as sheep pens.

Spaniards attempted to starve the Canarios out, only to be met by a hail of boulders which caused heavy casualties. Eventually a battle took place, with the Christians led by Pedro de Vera, assisted by Tenesor Semidan, the former king of Gáldar who had converted to the Spanish side with his followers. It was these Canarian "traitors" who saved the day for the Spanish. Although there were many deaths on both sides, the Guanches were defeated and forced to flee to their final stronghold at Fortaleza Grande near Santa Lucía (➤ 117).

All of this is explained at the small **museum** inside the **interpretation centre** for the Roque Bentaiga archaeological park. The captions are in Spanish but there is a booklet available in English, with detailed accounts of the historical and archaeological discoveries.

A **path** from the museum leads up towards the summit. The path is straightforward at first, but after a few minutes it runs out and the rest of the journey is rather a scramble.

TAKING A BREAK

The **museum café** sells drinks and snacks, but for a more substantial meal the nearest bars are in Tejeda.

🔡 178 C3 ✉ 4km southwest of Tejeda, signposted from C811

Centro de Interpretación
☎ 928 170384 🕐 Daily 10.30–5 💶 Inexpensive

5

Roque Nublo

It may not quite be the highest point on the island, but Roque Nublo (Cloud Rock) is undoubtedly the most emblematic of Gran Canaria's peaks. Its distinctive, slender silhouette can be seen from right across the sierra and the short climb on to the plateau makes a popular weekend walk.

The tall basalt monolith stands on a ridge above the village of **Ayacata**. The easiest way of getting there is to leave your car in the small car-park at La Goleta, on the minor road from Ayacata to Cruz de Tejeda. From here a wide trail heads towards the summit, passing the smaller figure of El Fraile (the friar), named after its resemblance to a praying monk.

There is a choice of paths to the **summit**, but the most direct route takes around 45 minutes each way. The climb is straightforward, but testing in places. Make sure you take plenty of water.

It begins with a **gentle ascent** through hillsides of euphorbia and broom, then grows steeper as you climb through the pinewoods beneath El Fraile. There are fine views over Ayacata, nestling in the valley to your left. After a succession of zigzags you come to a junction, where you could go straight ahead to make a complete circuit of the rock (see below). Instead, to reach the summit, take the higher path to your left. The path narrows as it ascends to a pass, where a rock-laid trail leads steeply to the plateau.

There are fine **views** from here, with the white town of Agaete to the northwest, and Tenerife on the horizon; and to

The climb to the summit of Roque Nublo begins on a well-marked path

The village of Tejeda sits in the shadow of Roque Nublo

the northeast the three distinctive hills of La Isleta in Las Palmas. To the east, terraced hillsides lead down to the village of La Culata, while behind you El Fraile and the car-park remind you how far you have climbed.

Up close, Roque Nublo appears much bigger than it does from a distance. It is actually 65m tall, and only serious climbers should attempt to scale the rock face.

For a **longer walk**, return to the pass beneath the plateau and turn right along a gravel path to make a complete circuit of the massif, enjoying views of Roque Nublo from every direction. The rule is simple – whenever there is a choice of paths, keep to the right. The path is easy, though there is plenty of vegetation so you may pick up a few scratches. The undulating path winds its way past boulders and through thickets of borage, broom and pine, passing beneath the northern face of

Roque Nublo, from where the rock appears to be balanced on its peak.

After around 30 minutes, a steep ascent leads back to the junction to rejoin the route to the car-park

Did You Know?
The white painted circle near the summit of Roque Nublo is said to mark the geographical centre of Gran Canaria.

The two monoliths at the summit are known as "father and son"

TAKING A BREAK
Drinks, fresh fruit and almond cake are available from a van in the **car-park**. There are also several roadside bars in nearby **Ayacata**.

➕ 178 C3

ROQUE NUBLO: INSIDE INFO

Top tips Try to arrive **early** in the day – the sun is less intense, the views are better and there is more space in the tiny car-park.

• Even in summer it can be **cold and windy** at the summit, so take a sweater or a warm jacket.

• To do this walk **without a car** you would need to take bus No 18 from San Fernando at 8am and walk up to Roque Nublo from Ayacata. The return bus leaves Ayacata at 4.45 pm. Make sure to check the bus times before you set out.

At Your Leisure

2 Cruz de Tejeda

A carved stone cross marks the notional centre of Gran Canaria at the top of this mountain pass (1,450m).

Cruz de Tejeda has always been something of a crossroads – for pilgrims, shepherds and trader – and these days it has a new role as

A close up view of the bell-tower on the Church of Our Lady in Tejeda

the commercial and tourist centre of the Central Mountains.

During the day, there is a bazaar-like atmosphere as coach parties descend on the square and the hawkers compete to offer them donkey rides or cheap souvenirs. At night, there is a very different atmosphere and you can wander among the Canary pines and chestnut trees enjoying views of Tenerife on one side and the plains of San Mateo on the other, or climb the path behind El Refugio Hotel (➤ 43) to watch the sun set over the sierra.

In addition to the hotel, there is a *parador* (state-run inn) designed in Canario style by Néstor Martín Fernández de la Torre in 1938. Unfortunately it has been closed for repairs for some time, but is expected to reopen in 2002 – check with the visitor centre.

Cruz de Tejeda is at the centre of the network of *caminos reales* (royal roads), with footpaths leading to Artenara, San Mateo and Teror.

Picnic Areas

The national environment agency ICONA has set up a number of road-side picnic areas in Gran Canaria. All of these are equipped with wooden tables and benches, and some have other facilities including barbecues, WCs, drinking water and children's playgrounds.

Among some of the most popular are:
Cueva de las Niñas (by the reservoir of the same name, southwest of Ayacata on the C811)
Llanos de la Paz (on the road from Roque Nublo to Cruz de Tejeda)
Montaña de Santiago (between Ayacata and the Chira reservoir)
Pinar de Tamadaba (in the pine woods near Artenara)

A short walk leads to the Mirador de Becerra, where there is a visitor centre devoted to the culture and landscape.
✚ 178 C4 ☎ Visitor centre 928 170336 ⏰ Daily 10–5 🚌 305 from Las Palmas

5 Tejeda

This quiet village of white houses at the head of the Barranco de Tejeda is overlooked by the vast Roque Bentaiga (► 110). The main street takes the form of a balcony, with a promenade giving views over the valley below. Most of the inhabitants live on the terraced slopes beneath the church square, where almonds and citrus fruits grow. In early spring-time the fields are carpeted with almond blossom, making a splendid sight and a good excuse for the festival El Almendro en Flor, usually held in the first week of February (► 120).
✚ 178 C3 🚌 305 from Las Palmas

6 Pico de las Nieves

At 1,949m above sea level, Pico de las Nieves (Snow Peak) is the highest point on Gran Canaria. The summit is

Sleepy San Bartolomé de Tirajana can be seen through the palm trees

used as a military base, but a lookout point just below the peak offers views over the sierra and the west of the island. Near the entrance to the military base is a recently restored well, Pozo de las Nieves, built by monks in 1699 in order to store the winter snows. The snow would be packed tightly beneath a layer of straw and when it turned to ice, it would be transferred to Las Palmas by mule for use in hospital operations in summer.
✚ 179 D3

7 San Bartolomé de Tirajana

It is sometimes hard to believe that this small rural township is the capital

Santa Lucía is a good place to soak up the atmosphere of rural Gran Canaria

of the municipality that controls the south coast resorts of Maspalomas and Playa del Inglés.

Life goes on at a gentle pace, and the biggest excitement is the Sunday morning market which takes place in the square around the 17th-century church. The same square contains the town hall, with wooden galleries and an attractive inner courtyard. The nearby bars sell *guindilla*, the local cherry brandy.

San Bartolomé stands at the head of the Barranco de Tirajana on the site of an earlier Guanche settlement known as Tunte. This is believed to have been a sacred site; when the conquerors came, they brought with them an image of St James, giving rise to the popular name for the town, Santiago de Tunte. From the *mirador* (lookout point) to the south of town there are views down the barranco all the way to the south coast.

🚩 179 D3 🚌 18 from Playa del Inglés, 34 from Agüimes

🗓 Santa Lucía

One of the prettiest villages on the island has become a magnet for the kind of rural tourism which Gran Canaria is hoping to attract. As you

Off the Beaten Track

The isolated village of **El Carrizal** clings to the steep slopes of a gorge above the Parralillo reservoir. The village bar has a terrace with views over the gorge, and the owner will rustle up something for you to eat in the church square. Nothing much grows here apart from palm trees and prickly pear and it's difficult to believe that anyone could live somewhere so remote, especially on a small island.

El Carrizal is reached by a snaking drive on a narrow road which leaves the C811 around 3km north of Ayacata. The road continues down to the reservoir, where you can turn right through a tunnel in the rock for the long climb to Artenara. To do this drive you need nerves of steel and a good hire car. The road is in good condition but is frequently affected by rockfalls, and there are few barriers in place to prevent you from crashing into the ravine. Use your horn on bends to warn other drivers of your presence.

For an equally spectacular drive, a left turn at the reservoir leads through the Barranco de la Aldea and down to the coast at San Nicolás de Tolentino.

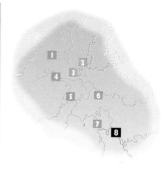

Petrol Stations

The only petrol stations in the mountain region are at Artenara, San Bartolomé de Tirajana, Santa Lucía and Tejeda.

wander around the village you come across wooden signs for *casas rurales* (cottages for rent) and *caminos* (footpaths), making this a suitable base for a holiday in the mountains, yet within easy reach of the coast.

Tourists visit Santa Lucía, yet few of them get further than the Museo Castillo de la Fortaleza, a mock castle in the gardens of the Hao restaurant (➤ 119). The castle houses a museum of Canarian life, with exhibits ranging from Roman amphorae and Guanche pottery to old weapons, farming implements and stuffed birds. Take your time to explore the rest of the village, with palm trees, gardens and an imposing white-domed neoclassical church.

South of Santa Lucía, a trail leads to Fortaleza Grande, a fortress-like rock which was the Guanches' final stronghold following their defeat at Roque Bentaiga (➤ 110) in 1483.

Guanche mummies are among the exhibits on display at the Museo Castillo de la Fortaleza

Ignoring the commands of their leader, Tenesor Semidan, to surrender to the Spanish conquerors, some of the 1,600 men and women who had retreated to this place threw themselves off the cliffs to their deaths.

➕ 179 D3 🚌 34 from Agüimes or San Bartolomé de Tirajana

Museo Castillo de la Fortaleza

✉ Calle Tomás Arroyo Cardosa ☎ 928 798007 🕐 Daily 9–5 💶 Inexpensive

Four Attractive Mountain Villages

- Cercados de Araña
- El Carrizal
- La Culata
- Las Lagunetas

Where to...
Eat and Drink

Prices
Expect to pay per person for a meal, excluding drinks and service
£ under 12 Euros ££ 12–24 Euros £££ over 24 Euros

Most restaurants on Gran Canaria are open throughout the year, though they may close for an annual holiday, usually in August.

ARTENARA

La Silla ££
In a village of cave houses, a cave restaurant comes as no surprise and you will not find a better setting than this. A gap in the mountains leads to a tunnel which emerges onto a sunny natural terrace beneath an overhanging rock with panoramic views of the central sierra. If the sun gets too hot, you can eat in one of several cool caves. The menu has Canarian cuisine with an emphasis on grilled meat, but the views are more interesting.

➕ 178 C4 🗺 Carretera La Silla 9
☎ 928 666108 🕐 Daily 10–6

CRUZ DE TEJEDA

El Refugio ££
Cruz de Tejeda is a very different place after dark when the restaurant in this hotel is the only place to eat. Most of the diners are hotel guests filling up after a walk in the mountains. The food is typically Canarian, filling and delicious.

➕ 178 C4 🗺 Cruz de Tejeda
☎ 928 666188 🕐 Daily noon–3, 8–10

Yolanda ££–£££
"*Cordero, cochinillo, cabrito, conejo, Canario*" ("lamb, suckling pig, goat, rabbit, Canario") reads the black-board, and this restaurant is all about hearty mountain cuisine. The speciality is roast meat – suckling pig is tender and crispy, served with potatoes and roasted pepper. Portions are huge and prices are not cheap. A terrace on the balcony offers views of Tenerife.

➕ 178 C4 🗺 Cruz de Tejeda
☎ 928 666276 🕐 Daily 9–7

SANTA LUCÍA

El Alpendre ££
You need to make an effort to seek out this place, hidden away on the edge of the Barranco de Tirajana on the side road leading to Fortaleza Grande. This is a genuine country restaurant, popular with locals. Steak is cooked over a roaring log fire. Eat at wooden benches out on the terrace, surrounded by the peace of the valley and the nearby hills.

➕ 179 D3 🗺 La Sorrueda
☎ 928 798449 🕐 Daily 1–4, 8–11
(closed Thu eve)

Hao ££
This is popular with tourists, but it is still a good place to try authentic Canarian cuisine, at heavy wooden tables with tree trunks for stools. Grills are the speciality, along with marinated olives, *patatas arrugadas* (▶ 19) and fresh goat's cheese. A shop sells liqueurs, herbal remedies and souvenirs. There is even a museum of Canarian life set inside a lake castle.

➕ 179 D3 🗺 Calle Tomás Arroyo Cardosa ☎ 928 798007
🕐 Daily 9–6

Where to...
Shop

There are few opportunities for shopping here, though T-shirts and souvenirs are sold from **roadside souvenir stalls** at Cruz de Tejeda. Other stalls feature local produce, almonds, almond cake, dried fruits and *bienmesabe* (almond syrup). In Tejeda, **Dulcería Nublo**, a pastry shop, sells almond biscuits and *mazapan* (almond cake).

Pottery, basketware and handwoven cloth are on sale at the **Centro de Recuperación Artesanal de la Cumbre**, set up in Artenara to revive and promote Canarian handicrafts. It is near the bus stop on the road to Tamadaba. Local pottery is available at the **Centro de Recuperación de Cerámica Tradicional Lugarejos**, an earthenware centre in the craft village Lugarejos (▲109).

Where to...
Be Entertained

FESTIVALS

El Almendro en Flor (early Feb): almond blossom festival takes place in Tejeda (▲116) with tastings of local produce.

San Isidro (15 May): agricultural fair in Artenara (P108) with music, dancing and folklore performances.

Fiesta de los Aborígenes (29 Apr): ceremonies are held at Fortaleza Grande near Santa Lucía (▲118) to mark the anniversary of the conquest of the island and the annexation of Gran Canaria by the Crown of Castile in 1483.

Santiago de Tunte (25 Jul): pilgrimages and religious processions in San Bartolomé de Tirajana (▲116) take place in honour of the patron saint.

La Virgen de la Cuevita (last Sun in Aug): folk dancing, fireworks and a procession in Artenara (▲108).

La Virgen del Socorro (15 Sep): an image of the Virgin is taken down from the church in Tejeda (▲116) and paraded around the town by participants.

Santa Lucía (13 Dec): this Swedish winter festival brings together Scandinavian and Canarian traditions and a week of street parties in honour of the patron saint of Santa Lucía (▲117).

OUTDOOR ACTIVITIES

Walking, cycling, fishing and hunting are all popular leisure activities in the Central Mountains, which offer stunning scenery.

The best **walking** is along the restored network of *caminos reales* (royal roads), footpaths and mule tracks which were once the main routes across the island. Walking maps and guides can be bought at the government bookshop in Las Palmas (▲74). **Rutas Canarias** (▲150) offers guided mountain walks, including one from Cruz de Tejeda to Artenara. Conditions in the mountains are more changeable than on the coast, and you will need extra clothing as well as food, water and good shoes.

Fishing is possible in the reservoirs of Chira and Cueva de las Niñas, though you will need to obtain a licence. Ask where to get one at the nearest tourist office.

Spectator sports

The El Corte Ingles **rally-driving** event takes place over two days in March or April on a circuit which includes Ayacata, Artenara and Cruz de Tejeda, tel: 928 383887; www.bme.es/racortin.

The South

Getting Your Bearings

The Gran Canaria of the holiday brochures begins in San Agustín and follows an arc around the south coast to Puerto de Mogán. This is a land of golden beaches and sunny skies. The trade winds and clouds that blow across the north of the island stack up in the Central Mountains, so the south coast basks in year-round sunshine. In winter you can be sunbathing on the beaches while snow is visible on the hills.

Puerto de la Aldea **11**

San Nicolás de Tolentino

Punta Bermejo

Tocodomán

Playa de Güigüí **10**

Tasártico

Tasarte

El Descojonado

Playa del Asno **10**

Mogán

Playa de Tasarte

Punta del Cerrillo

Playa de Veneguera **10**

Puerto de Mogán **9**

Taurito

Playa de Taurito

Playa de Tauro

Puerto Rico

Despite the attractions of Las Palmas and the growth of inland tourism, the vast majority of visitors to Gran Canaria stay on the south coast. Many people arrive at the airport and head straight down to the coast for their holiday, finding that a single resort meets all of their needs. Each of the resorts has its own particular character – young or old, chic or cheerful, sporty or sedate. Puerto Rico appeals to families and watersports enthusiasts, San Agustín to older couples, and Playa del Inglés to the party-loving crowd. Maspalomas and Puerto de Mogán are fashionable and upmarket. In some places, tourism has undoubtedly scarred the landscape, but in others, such as the villas of Puerto de Mogán or the serried ranks of apartment blocks at Puerto Rico, it has contributed new and dramatic landscapes of its own.

You don't have to go far inland to experience a very different Gran Canaria. Peaceful towns and villages such as Agüimes and Fataga, and monumental *barrancos* (gorges) that sweep down the mountains to the sea, are all just a short drive away. Even

on the wild west coast beyond Puerto de Mogán, it is still possible to discover an isolated beach and a glimpse of Gran Canaria as it used to be.

Timeshares

In the resorts on the south coast you might find timeshare touts offering you free trips or prizes if you attend a demonstration. Don't worry – a polite refusal is usually enough to see them off.

0   8 km
0   5 miles

1 Barranco de Guayadeque

Cuevas Bermejas
El Altillo
Santa Lucía
Ingenio
Carrizal

2 Agüimes

C815

C815

Punta de la Sal

Cruce de Sardina

Arteara
Sardina
Arinaga

Palmitos Parque 6

Barranco de 5 Fataga

Hoya de Toledo

El Doctoral
Bahía Feliz
Punta Tenefe

Juan Grande

GCI
C812
La Caleta

San Agustín
Punta del Tarajalillo

Playa de San Agustín

Playa del Inglés

3 Playa del Inglés

Maspalomas

4 Dunas de Maspalomas

Punta de Maspalomas

El Tablero

Playa de guinguín

7 Arguine-guín

Las Meloneras
Playa de las Meloneras
El Oasis
Playa de Maspalomas

Page 121: The spectacular Dunas de Maspalomas

The two sides of Puerto Rico – Playa de los Amadores (left) and the harbour (above)

From beaches to *barrancos*, this tour reveals the south of Gran Canaria in all its unexpected variety.

Southern Gran Canaria in Two Days

Day One

Morning

Take the road from Agüimes into the **Barranco de Guayadeque** (➤ 126) to experience the natural splendour and unique character of this gorge (left). After coffee in the village of **Cuevas Bermejas** (➤ 127), continue to the end of the road for lunch at **Tagoror** (➤ 145).

Afternoon

Leaving the valley, take time for a brief stroll around the old quarter of **Agüimes** (➤ 140) before driving down to the coast at **Playa del Inglés** (➤ 129). The quickest and most direct route is on the GC1 motorway, but a more scenic alternative is the twisting mountain drive through Santa Lucía and the **Barranco de Fataga** (➤ 140). Arriving in Playa del Inglés, head straight down to the beach for a promenade along the Paseo Costa Canaria, followed by a sunset stroll across the **Dunas de Maspalomas** (below, ➤ 132).

Evening

After dinner at a beachside restaurant, check out the action in the **Kasbah**, **Metro** and **Yumbo centres** (➤ 148), the liveliest places to be at midnight and beyond.

Day Two

Morning

Allow yourself a couple of hours to wander around **Palmitos Parque** (➤ 136), taking in the bird of prey and parrot shows (above) before a light lunch at the terrace café.

Afternoon

If you have children, take them to **Aqua Sur** (on the same road as Palmitos Parque) (➤ 136) to spend the afternoon enjoying the wave pools, waterslides and lazy river. Alternatively, take the old coast road through **Arguineguín** (➤ 141) and spend an hour or two topping up your tan on the beach at **Puerto Rico** (left, ➤ 142).

Evening

Continue on the coast road to **Puerto de Mogán** (right, ➤ 138) for a drink beside the harbour while the sun sets behind the cliffs. After a walk around the marina, have your evening meal here, and enjoy the fresh local fish at **La Cofradía de Pescadores** (➤ 146).

O

Barranco de Guayadeque

Not far from the crowded beaches of the south coast, there are people who still live in caves and tend their goats much as their ancestors must have done before the Spanish arrived. In this spectacular gorge between Agüimes and Ingenio, the spiritual descendants of the Guanches are doing their best to keep alive the pre-Hispanic lifestyle of Gran Canaria.

The Barranco de Guayadeque slices across the landscape from the high mountains down to the coast. Its Guanche name means "a place of running water", and it was once a riverbed filled with reeds. It is still home to some 80 endemic species of **flora**, including a native variety of rock-rose, and Canary palms and euphorbia grow on the valley floor. The entire

The road to Guayadeque follows the valley floor

The small cave chapel in the village of Cuevas Bermejas

gorge has now been designated a nature reserve and archaeological park.

Many of the exhibits in the Museo Canario in Las Palmas (➤ 56) were discovered in Guayadeque, and it is clear that this was the site of a significant **Guanche settlement**. The earliest inhabitants built cave houses on the sunny, eastern side of the valley and burial caves for their dead on the shady western side. As you enter the canyon, you can make out some of the entrances to the caves high in the valley walls. Most of them are inaccessible except by a steep and difficult climb.

A paved road from Agüimes leads down to the valley floor, soon reaching the village of **Cuevas Bermejas** (scarlet caves), where several cave dwellings have been carved into a cliff face of red volcanic rock. Opposite the car-park, a path climbs the hillside towards the cave houses, many of which have modern amenities such as solar panels and TV aerials. Patios, pets and window-boxes overflowing with plants complete the domestic scene. Some of the villagers keep their cars in cave garages, while others use the caves as shelters for goats and chickens, climbing the hillside each day to the pastureland on the higher plateau. A pair of cave bars in the village serve snacks such as olives and *papas arrugadas* (➤ 19), and there is a simple chapel hewn out of the rock. The names of the gods may have changed and living here may now be a lifestyle choice rather than a necessity, but the people of Cuevas Bermejas are perhaps the closest living relatives of the 15th-century aborigines of Gran Canaria.

Beyond Cuevas Bermejas, the walls rise to a height of 300m and terraced fields of almonds begin to appear on the slopes, carpeting the valley with a layer of white blossom in spring. There is a roadside picnic area at **Montaña de las Tierras**, with benches, tables and barbecues in the shade of two eucalyptus trees. A little further on, the road runs out at **Tagoror** (➤ 145), a famous restaurant set inside a series of caves high above the gorge. A footpath from the restaurant leads to another hamlet of cave houses, even more isolated than the first.

You cannot take a car further than this, but **walkers** can continue on the road which climbs through almond and olive groves and forests of Canary pine towards the centre of the island. This is a magnificent route but it should only be attempted by experienced walkers with a good map or guide.

TAKING A BREAK

The cave bars at **Cuevas Bermejas** are good for a drink and a snack, but **Tagoror** (➤ 145) is the best place for lunch.

➕ 179 D3 🚍 11, 21, 34 to Agüimes then take a taxi

Cave houses are warm in winter and cool in summer

BARRANCO DE GUAYADEQUE: INSIDE INFO

Top tip Come here on a Sunday, when the restaurant **Tagoror** serves *sancocho* (Canarian fish stew) and the valley floor fills up with families enjoying a picnic lunch or an impromptu barbecue in the barranco.

Hidden gem Coming out of the valley, don't miss the opportunity for a stroll around the old town of **Agüimes** (➤ 140).

In more depth You can explore the upper reaches of the gorge in more detail on a **guided walk** which takes place each Friday. The walk begins at Pico de las Nieves (➤ 116) and descends for around 10km into the Barranco de Guayadeque. Meet at 10 am outside the tourist office in Playa del Inglés (➤ 131), where minibus transport is provided to the start of the walk. More details can be obtained from *Rutas Canarias* (tel: 689 775034).

3

Playa del Inglés

The dusty tomato fields of Playa del Inglés have been transformed into the setting for the richest cash crop Gran Canaria has ever known – tourism. Even if you are not staying here, it is essential to visit to see what tourism has done for Gran Canaria. The once barren clifftops are now a non-stop holiday playground, as big and brash as anything you will find on Tenerife, Mallorca or the Spanish costas. The "English beach" has become an international party circuit of Swedish restaurants and German bars, with hotels, apartment blocks, bungalows, shopping centres, playgrounds, mini-golf courses and nightclubs catering for the whims of a year-round stream of visitors.

Jet-skiing is one of many watersports on offer on the island

The Paseo Costa Canaria looks out over the real glory of Playa del Inglés. The **beach** of fine golden sand stretches for more than 5km, bordering the Dunas de Maspalomas (► 132) for much of the way. Watersports, pedal boats, parasols and sunbeds are all available and there are restaurants and bars.

The central part of the beach is always crowded, but it is usually possible to find a quieter spot, particularly if you head for the long stretch of nudist beach between Maspalomas and Playa del Inglés. The Paseo (promenade) itself makes for an enjoyable stroll, especially at sunset, and forms the central

Beach bars cater for an international clientele

section of a longer walk along the south coast (➤ 158). You can walk directly onto the dunes from the beaches at Maspalomas and Playa del Inglés, or from the *mirador* behind the Riu Palace Maspalomas Hotel (➤ 43).

Most people who stay here find that Playa del Inglés provides everything they want from their holiday, although some may consider it a rather artificial place, without the historic old quarter or central square that acts as a focus for most Spanish towns. The **plazas**, where people meet, are inside the *centros comerciales* (shopping centres), the biggest of which is Cita, though Yumbo (where the tourist office is situated) is perhaps the best known and the Kasbah is the focus of young nightlife.

Close to the Kasbah, an attempt has been made to create a heart for the resort with the opening of the ecumenical **church of San Salvador** in 1971. The church is built in the shape of a ship, with a twisted wrought-iron façade symbolising a divided Christian church, and an altar hewn out of red volcanic rock. Services are held in English, German and Spanish.

Playa del Inglés is the biggest resort in a conurbation which stretches from San Agustín to Maspalomas and beyond. In recent years this area has been successfully rebranded as the **Costa Canaria**, in an effort to dispel some of the negative connotations of the "English beach". In fact each resort has its own particular flavour. San Agustín is old-fashioned and upmarket, Playa del Inglés is young and upfront, while Las Meloneras, beyond the lighthouse at Maspalomas, is a luxury holiday village featuring chic hotels, a conference centre, golf course, marina and shopping mall. San Fernando, inland from Playa del Inglés, is where the people who work in the industry live. This is the place to go if you want a slice

Conde de la Vega Grande

Much of the development of this area is due to the vision of one man, Alejandro del Castillo, Conde de la Vega Grande, who turned his estates into the first tourist developments along the south coast. Depending on your point of view, the count is either the hero or the villain of tourism in Gran Canaria. His efforts unleashed a building boom which lasted through the 1960s and 1970s, the results of which can be seen around Playa del Inglés. This is a place of high-rise buildings and wide boulevards, whose names (Inglaterra, Alemania, Francia, Italia, Finlandia, Estados Unidos) pay tribute to the resort's international clientele. Unfortunately the only pleasant place for walking is along the seafront promenade.

of authentic Spanish life, with neighbourhood shops and tapas bars frequented by locals as much as tourists.

TAKING A BREAK

There are restaurants and bars all over the resort, particularly in the shopping centres, behind the beach and along Avenida de Tirajana. For something authentically Spanish try **Las Cumbres** (▶ 145).

🚻 179 D1 🚌 1, 4, 5, 25, 29, 30, 32, 36, 45, 61, 66, 72, 90

Tourist information office

The church of San Salvador has services in three different languages

🚻 185 D4 ✉ Yumbo Centre ☎ 928 771550 🕐 Mon–Fri 9–9, Sat 9–2

Templo Ecuménico de San Salvador

🚻 185 E4 ✉ Plaza de Maspalomas ☎ 928 760603 🕐 Daily 6–9.30 pm (plus services at weekends) 🎟 Free

---

PLAYA DEL INGLÉS: INSIDE INFO

Top tips Pick up a **local bus map** from the tourist office at the Yumbo centre.
• Walking around the resort can be quite tiring and **buses** make a good alternative.

❹
Dunas de Maspalomas

Eerie, surreal, almost lunar in their simplicity, these Sahara-like sand dunes at the southernmost tip of the island are one of the scenic highlights of Gran Canaria.

These undulating hills and valleys cover an area of 4sq km between Maspalomas and Playa del Inglés. The sand is composed of finely ground shells, left behind when the sea retreated at the end of the Ice Age. There are few more memorable experiences than walking barefoot across the hot

Follow the footprints across the shifting sands

Parasols and sunbeds can be hired on the beach

sand and watching the dunes change shape as each new gust of wind creates intricate patterns in the sandscape.

Although access to the dunes is unrestricted, they form part of a protected **nature reserve** and it is essential not to pick plants, disturb wildlife or move stones. Sunbathing, however, is permitted and you will notice that the area is popular with naturists and gay men. Camel rides are available from the safari centre on the western edge of the dunes, though environmentalists disapprove of them, claiming that they have an adverse impact on the fragile ecosystem.

Maspalomas beach is a popular spot. The landmark here is the lighthouse, **Faro de Maspalomas**, which at 56m is the tallest in the Canaries. A promenade leads to **Las Meloneras**, a

sheltered bay once frequented by locals but now the site of a luxury holiday resort complete with shopping mall, marina and a traditional Canarian village.

The neighbouring resort of **Maspalomas** is low-rise and chic, with bungalows and villas set around well-maintained gardens. Much of the accommodation is behind the golf course in the district of Campo Internacional, where the avenues are named after the tour operators who have brought so much prosperity to this region.

The **Faro 2** shopping centre, the heart of the resort, is also situated here.

Maspalomas beach has undergone many changes in recent years. When the lighthouse was built in 1886, Maspalomas could only be reached by a dirt track and most of the supplies had to be brought in by boat. The first plans for tourist development came in the 1950s, with proposals for a *parador* (state-run hotel), zoo and racetrack on what was described as an "isolated

La Charca

At the west end of the dunes, La Charca is a sea-water and freshwater lagoon with reed beds and marshes which play host to a wide variety of nesting and migratory birds.

Kestrel, grey heron, seagulls and Kentish plover are all regularly seen here, and the Sardinian warbler nests in the tamarisk groves between February and June. Mullet are found in La Charca at high tide, lizards scramble about the banks and osprey are occasionally spotted searching for fish at dusk. At the mouth of the lagoon, a grove of Canary palm trees extends westward into the area known as El Oasis, home to some of the island's top hotels.

beach". The landowner, Conde de la Vega Grande (➤ 130), rejected the plans in favour of large-scale construction, and the battle for the dunes began.

A golf course, opened in 1968, encroached onto the dunes and the notorious Hotel Dunas was built on the sand before being demolished in 1989.

Ecologists are continuing to campaign against beach bars and camel shelters, but the Dunas de Maspalomas are better protected now than since tourism began and a balance has finally been struck between the conflicting interests of profit and preservation.

Further inland, **Sonnenland** is a new tourist area with views over the dunes, while **El Tablero** is the Canarian quarter of Maspalomas, a village-like suburb on the far side of the motorway with a distinctly Spanish atmosphere.

Take a camel ride and you might think you're in the Sahara

TAKING A BREAK

The nearest restaurants are in the **Oasis shopping centre** in the lanes behind Maspalomas beach. The lunchtime buffet at **La Foresta** (➤ 145) at the Maspalomas Oasis hotel is a good deal.

➕ 179 D1   🚌 5, 25, 29, 30, 36, 44, 50, 70, 90

Tourist information office
✉ Mirador Campo de Golf (between Campo Internacional and Playa del Inglés) ☎ 928 769585 🕐 Mon–Fri 9–9, Sat 9–2

DUNAS DE MASPALOMAS: INSIDE INFO

Top tips Take plenty of **water** if you plan to walk across the dunes as the combination of sun and sand can be very dehydrating. It is generally easier to walk barefoot. For more advice on walking across the dunes, see the Costa Canaria walk (➤ 158).

• Beyond the Faro de Maspalomas (lighthouse), **Playa de las Mujeres** is a rocky beach with good conditions for surfing and windsurfing.

• One of the best **views** of the dunes is at sunset from the terrace of the Ruiu Palace Maspalomas Hotel in Playa del Inglés (➤ 44).

In more depth The **information centre** for the Dunas de Maspalomas nature reserve has a permanent exhibition on the history and ecology of the dunes. It is situated in Playa del Inglés, behind the Riu Palace Maspalomas hotel by the *mirador* overlooking the dunes. The centre is open Monday to Saturday 9–2.

You can use the lighthouse to guide your way as you walk across the dunes

6

Palmitos Parque

The squawking of parrots in a verdant valley of palm trees forms the scenic backdrop to Gran Canaria's most popular family attraction. This subtropical park inside the Barranco de Chamoriscán has more than 200 species of birds, including macaws, toucans, hornbills, flamingoes, cockatiels, peacocks and cranes. Among the other attractions are cactus gardens, an orchid house, a butterfly house and an aquarium.

The park manages to strike a balance between education, conservation and entertainment. Most visitors head straight for the **parrot shows**, which take place every hour from 11 am on a café terrace near the entrance. The parrots have been trained to perform an amazing variety of tricks, from riding bicycles to doing jigsaws, painting pictures and counting to ten. They have even learned how to imitate foreign visitors, lying back on a parrot-size deckchair reading a newspaper. Children love it, most adults may feel slightly uncomfortable, yet the fact is that such popular displays help to fund serious conservation programmes among the many endangered species which exist in the park.

It is best to follow the **signs** around the park to see everything in the suggested order. The complete circuit takes about an hour of leisurely walking, but you should allow half a day. Don't miss the excellent **birds of prey show** which takes place twice daily (12.30 and 3.30) on a hilltop overlooking the park, where eagles, owls and peregrine falcons swoop down over the audience in free flight. Other highlights are the **cactus**

It's not just for parrots – the park also features butterflies and plants

garden with its numerous cactus and aloe plants, among them the *silla de la suegra* or "mother-in-law's chair"; the **aquarium** with sea-water and freshwater tanks of tropical fish; and the **gibbon island**, home to a pair of gibbons.

A shop at the exit sells colourful souvenirs such as T-shirts and stuffed toy parrots, and there is also the opportunity to have your photo taken with a pair of screeching macaws.

TAKING A BREAK

There are **cafés** and ice-cream kiosks scattered throughout the park, and a **self-service terrace** near the exit which serves reasonably priced soup, salads and hot meals. Alternatively, take a **picnic**.

A well-marked trail leads visitors around the park

✚ 178 C2 ✉ Carretera de los Palmitos, 15km northwest of Playa del Inglés
☎ 928 140276 ⏲ Daily 9.30–6 🚌 45, 70 💶 Expensive

PALMITOS PARQUE: INSIDE INFO

Top tips There are regular **buses** to Palmitos Parque from Playa del Inglés, departing every 15 minutes during the morning and every 30 minutes during the afternoon. There are also four buses each morning from Puerto Rico and Maspalomas, returning in the afternoon.

• **Children** love Palmitos Parque, but there is a fair amount of walking involved, so it is best to take a pushchair for younger children.

• Pick up a **plant guide** at the entrance to help you to identify the various plants on display.

Hidden gem Don't miss the **hummingbirds** as you leave the park. These tiny birds with their bright plumage and unbelievably fast wing movements live in a series of small cages near the exit.

In more depth Climb the hill behind the park for good **views** over the valley. Beyond a hotel, the dusty footpath leads eventually to the reservoir at Ayagaures, inside the Barranco de la Data.

🔟

Puerto de Mogán

An enticing blend of fishing village, marina and chic holiday resort, Puerto de Mogán is often held up as a model of sympathetic tourist development in Gran Canaria. Low-rise villas with hand-painted borders and gardens of hibiscus and bougainvillea form a gentle backdrop to the harbour, where Venetian-style bridges arch over sea-water canals. The tallest building is the four-storey harbourmaster's tower, built in the same distinctive style. For many people, the fact that this is the only south coast resort without a *centro comercial* (shopping mall) speaks volumes.

This is the farthest place on the island from Las Palmas and (for the moment) it marks the western limit of tourism. Puerto de Mogán was not developed for tourism until the 1980s, with the result that it was able to avoid some of the excesses of its neighbours along the coast. Right from the start, this was a small-scale, exclusive resort, designed for the sort of people who could afford a berth in the harbour. Others have to make do with seeing Puerto de Mogán on a day trip by boat from Puerto Rico (➤ 142).

Most people come here just to wander around the quayside, admiring the yachts and the fishing vessels and enjoying the **view** from the waterfront cafés.

For something more active, diving, sailing and fishing trips are all on offer, and an added attraction is a journey on the **Yellow Submarine**, a 45-minute voyage to the bottom of the ocean to observe marine life and the wreck of an old freighter

lying 20m below the surface (for bookings and information, tel: 928 565108).

From the small sandy beach you can see **Playa de Taurito**, a sharp contrast to Puerto de Mogán. Here, high-rise hotels have grown up around landscaped gardens and a sea-water lake in a ravine between the cliffs.

A road leads inland along the floor of the **Barranco de Mogán**, a tropical valley where mangoes, avocados and papaya are grown. Outsize coffee pots, stools and household utensils line the road, kept here throughout the year and transported on carriages in a ritual procession during the feast of San Antonio de Padua each June (➤ 149). After 12km the road reaches **Mogán**, a county town in the shadow of the Guirre mountain. The main sight here is the church of San Antonio, containing a fine hand-carved wooden coffered ceiling.

These are a far cry from the apartment blocks of Playa del Inglés

Cactualdea Cactus Park

This unusual park near Tocodomán (tel: 928 891228, open daily 10–6, moderate) combines an impressive cactus garden with tourist attractions including a model Guanche cave, a wine cellar and a carillon which plays *Don't Cry For Me Argentina*. There is an amphitheatre with displays of pole-vaulting and Canarian wrestling. The restaurant serves typical Canarian cuisine. As well as cacti, the gardens have palm and dragon trees and are well worth a visit if you cannot make it to the Jardín Canario (➤ 85).

TAKING A BREAK

Keep walking around the marina until you come to the fishing harbour, where **La Cofradía de Pescadores** (➤ 146) serves fresh local fish. The nearby **El Faro** is a popular restaurant in a lighthouse at the end of the quay.

Left: Chic and cheerful – the harbour at Puerto de Mogán

🚩 178 B2 🚌 1, 32, 61 from Las Palmas/Playa del Inglés, 84 from Puerto de Mogán to Mogán

At Your Leisure

2 Agüimes

The historic centre of this town, once the seat of the bishops of Gran Canaria, has been sympathetically restored as a model of the new, inland tourism which the island is trying so hard to promote. The narrow streets around the main square, **Plaza del Rosario**, are full of old-style, whitewashed houses, several of them converted into holiday homes. The plaza is dominated by the neo-classical church of San Sebastián, a former cathedral with sculptures by Canarian artist, Luján Pérez. Agüimes is a thriving town with a strong Canarian identity, and a commitment to the arts which embraces international festivals of drama, storytelling and music (➤ 149).

The nearby sand and pebble beach at **Arinaga** is good for windsurfing and is the venue for a festival of world music each summer.

➕ 183 E3 🚌 11, 34

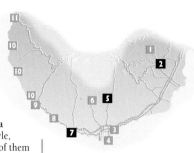

A walk around the old quarter of Agüimes offers a chance to explore a different side of Gran Canaria

5 Barranco de Fataga

The biggest gorge on Gran Canaria is also one of the most dramatic, with palm-filled oases, walls of honey-coloured rock, and canyon-like scenery that conjures up images of Wild West films.

The road into the gorge begins in Playa del Inglés and for visitors staying on the south coast the drive up to Fataga is the easiest way to get a brief taste of Gran Canaria's mountain scenery. The first stop is **Mundo Aborigen**, an open-air theme park devoted to the Guanche way of life. Although it lacks the scholarship of the Museo Canario (➤ 56), the park gives genuine insight into the pre-Hispanic culture of Gran Canaria, brought to life through a series of tableaux and the chronicles of the early Spanish conquistadors. There are reproductions of stone houses, burial caves, a convent and a meeting place, and vivid descriptions of everything from surgery to execution.

Just north of here, a bend in the road is the setting for a magnificent *mirador*, with views over the canyon and back towards the coast. There is a bar and a small car-park where you can get out and stretch your legs while taking in the views.

The road continues to **Arteara**, where camel rides are offered in the oasis. At the end of the village, a short climb up a cactus-covered hillside

leads to a Guanche necropolis, where many of the tombs are still intact.

After more twists and turns you arrive in **Fataga**, extensively restored as a showpiece village of traditional Canarian houses surrounded by orchards and palm trees. There are several bars and cafés. The German artist Friedhelm Berghorn has a studio at the top of the village and there are craft and souvenir shops on the main road. The shady square in front of the church makes a good place to relax and prepare yourself for the hair-raising drive back down the gorge.

➕ 178 D2

Mundo Aborigen
✉ Carretera de Fataga, km6 ☎ 928 172295 🕐 Daily 9–6 🍴 Café and snack bar inexpensive 🚌 18 from Playa del Inglés 🎟 Expensive

🟥 Arguineguín
Until recently this small town at the end of the motorway was little more than a fishing village. It is still a work-ing fishing port, with smacks tied up in the harbour, a shrine to the Virgin of Fishermen, several good seafood restaurants and some lively fisher-men's bars, but it has gradually expanded to become a mass-market resort popular with Germans and Scandinavians.

A coastal promenade connects Arguineguín to Patalavaca where luxury hotels and apartments are

It is highly advisable to keep your eye on the road and not on the scenery as you follow the twisting, turning drive into the Barranco de Fataga

Boat Trips
Puerto Rico is the starting point for a number of boat trips. They can all be booked through tour operators or at the desks in the harbour. The cheapest are the Lineas Salmón ferry services, which depart eight times a day for Puerto de Mogán and four times daily for Arguineguín, with extra trips on market days.

Several companies offer dolphin-watching cruises from Puerto Rico, including *Spirit of the Sea* (tel: 928 562229), whose two-hour trip on a glass-bottomed catamaran uses sophisticated searching equipment, though sightings are not guaranteed.

Daytime and sunset cruises, with food, drink, entertainment and swimming included, are available on the schooner *Timanfaya* (tel: 928 762696) and the windjammer *San Miguel* (tel: 928 760076).

For a more laid-back cruise, the 30m *Super Cat* (tel: 928 150248) catamaran sails daily up the west coast to Güigüi.

Another option is a complete round-the-island tour with Armas (tel: 928 474545) on a ship which departs three times a week from the harbour at Arguineguín.

Off the Beaten Track

The road into the Barranco de Arguineguín begins opposite a banana plantation where the C812 coast road divides from the motorway. Passing a campsite and the village of Cercado Espino, it climbs into a fertile valley of tropical fruits around the hamlet of Barranquillo de San Andrés. A right fork leads to Soria, where the village bar Casa Fernando serves fresh papaya juice and Canarian tapas. From here you can walk down to the dam overlooking the Soria reservoir, built in 1971 to provide water for the south coast resorts. The road through Soria quickly deteriorates into a dusty track; if you have an off-road vehicle, you can continue for 8km to Cruce de la Data, returning through Ayacata and the Barranco de Fataga.

springing up around the beaches and coves and **Anfi del Mar**, an upmarket timeshare resort with a beach of imported Caribbean sand. The walk takes around an hour.

Arguineguín is busy every Tuesday as it hosts one of the region's biggest **markets**. The best way to avoid the traffic is to take one of the regular

Puerto Rico has been built up over the past 30 years – and there don't seem to be any plans to stop

boat services from Puerto Rico or Puerto de Mogán for a stroll around the harbour and lunch on the quay.

🚌 178 C1 🚍 1, 61, 91 from Las Palmas; 32 from Playa del Inglés and Puerto de Mogán

🔟 Puerto Rico

The first sight of Puerto Rico takes your breath away. Rows of white apartment blocks climb up the steep hillsides, so high that you need a taxi to get to the top and there is even talk of putting in a cable car.

The resort is especially popular with British families. As it was only built in the 1970s, there is no historic centre, but its heart is the large park inside the *barranco*, planted with palm and ficus trees and featuring mini-golf courses, tennis courts, a playground and a heated pool. The main shopping centre is just behind the park, and there is another at the top of the hill.

The beach is a crescent of golden sand imported from the Sahara. The sand shelves gently into the sea, making it perfect for young children. From the harbours to either side of

the beach, boards
advertise fishing trips,
watersports, cruises
and ferries to Puerto
de Mogán (► 138).
A clifftop path leads in
around 20 minutes to
Playa de los Amadores,
where there is another
glorious man-made beach.
From the path there are good
sunset views over Tenerife. (Tourist
information ► 37.)

🚌 178 B1 🚍 1, 61, 91 from Las
Palmas; 32 from Playa del Inglés and
Puerto de Mogán

🔟 West Coast Beaches

The remote beaches of the southwest
coast are largely untouched by
tourism, though after a long legal and
political battle **Playa de Veneguera**
has been sold to developers and will
be transformed into a mega-resort by
2010. At the moment it can only be
reached by a 10km dirt track through
orchards and banana plantations, and
is inaccessible without an off-road
vehicle. Seek out this lonely beach of
black sand before it is too late.

North of here, **Playa de Tasarte** is
situated at the mouth of a *barranco*

For Kids

Although the children may be happy just playing on the beach, there are also other
attractions. The top draw for families is **Palmitos Parque** (► 136), though **Cocodrilo
Park** near Agüimes (tel: 928 784725, open Mon–Fri and Sun 10–5) features croco-
dile and parrot shows and also has tigers, monkeys and deer. Or try the **Mundo
Aborigen** (► 140) and **Sioux City** (► 144) theme parks, and the ride on the *Yellow
Submarine* at Puerto de Mogán (► 138). **Aqua Sur** waterpark (tel: 928 560666,
open daily 10–6), on the road to Palmitos Parque, has slides, rides and thrills, as
do **Aquapark** at Puerto Rico (tel: 928 560666, open daily 10–6)and **Ocean Park**
at Maspalomas (tel: 928 764361, open daily 10–6). **Holiday World**, in the Campo
Internacional area of Maspalomas (tel: 928 767171, open daily 6 pm–midnight),
is an old-fashioned funfair and amusement park which is undergoing a much-
needed facelift.

and has the advantage that it can be reached by a tarmac road. A simple fish restaurant on the seafront is popular with locals at weekends.

The best of all the remote beaches is **Güigüi** (pronounced *wee-wee*), which can only be reached by a 3-hour hike over the mountains from Tasártico or by boat from Puerto Rico. It is a protected nature reserve and perhaps the most idyllic spot in Gran Canaria.

Ⅲ Puerto de la Aldea

This small fishing village is also the port for the tomato town of **San Nicolás de Tolentino**, 5km inland. There is a long pebble beach with good surf at its southern end, and a small sheltered beach of dark sand beneath overhanging rocks by the harbour. There are a couple of good fish restaurants at the end of the promenade.

Puerto de la Aldea is Gran Canaria's westernmost point and it can feel quite wild in winter when the wind gets up. The lagoon at the southern end of the beach is the

setting for one of Gran Canaria's oldest festivals, **Fiesta del Charco** (➤ 149).

➕ 178 A4 ➡️ 38, 101 from Las Palmas to San Nicolás via south and north coasts respectively

Sioux City

Set in a canyon just outside San Agustín, Sioux City is a Wild West theme town featuring shoot-outs, riding displays, saloons, can-can girls and evening barbecue shows for large parties of tourists. The scenery here is so like Arizona that several Westerns have been filmed in the area (Cañon del Águila, San Agustín, tel: 928 762573, open Tue–Sun 10–5 (shows at noon, 1.30, 3 and 4.30), bus No 29 from Maspalomas/Playa del Inglés, expensive).

The pebble beach at Puerto de la Aldea is an excellent place to enjoy a lunch of freshly caught fish

Where to...
Eat and Drink

Prices
Expect to pay per person for a meal, excluding drinks and service
£ under 12 Euros ££ 12–24 Euros £££ over 24 Euros

Most restaurants on Gran Canaria are open throughout the year, though they may close for an annual holiday, usually in August.

BARRANCO DE GUAYADEQUE

Tagoror ££
The most memorable feature of this restaurant is its setting in several cool caves high above the *barranco*. Eat outside on a charming vine-covered terrace. The food is typically Canarian – grilled meats, spicy potatoes, *morcilla* sausage and local *quesos* (cheeses). Desserts include fried bananas with *bienmesabe* (almond syrup). It gets very busy at weekends and on Sunday when locals gather to eat traditional *sancocho* (fish stew).

➕ 179 D4 ⊠ Montaña de las Tierras
📞 928 172013 🕓 Daily 10 am–2 am

PLAYA DEL INGLÉS

Casa Pepe El Breca II £££
This offshoot of a Las Palmas fish restaurant is run for many years by the same family. It is found in a typical Canarian house on the road to Fataga, right on top of the GC1 motorway. There are a few tables in the garden, but you need to book ahead or arrive early to be sure of one of these. There is usually no menu – the waiter will guide you to a selection of fish-dominated tapas followed by the fresh fish of the day – grilled or baked in a salt crust. If you would prefer to eat meat, say so.

➕ 185 D5 ⊠ Lomo Maspalomas, Carretera de Fataga 📞 928 772637
🕓 Mon–Sat 1–4, 7–midnight

Las Cumbres ££
With so much bland international cuisine on offer, this distinctively Spanish cellar restaurant in the heart of Playa del Inglés is quite a surprise. Shepherds' crooks, sheeps' bells and goathorns give a clue to the speciality – roast lamb. The main influence comes from La Rioja, which can be seen in dishes like roast peppers and salt cod – Riojan style, but other Spanish regions are represented with Andalusian *gazpacho* (chilled tomato soup), and Catalan custard for dessert.

➕ 185 D3 ⊠ Edificio Taida, Avenida de Tirajana 📞 928 760941
🕓 Wed–Mon 1–4, 7–midnight

MASPALOMAS

La Foresta ££–£££
Non-residents are welcome at the poolside restaurant of the Maspalomas Oasis Hotel, and the lunchtime buffet is good value. The full menu will leave quite a hole in your wallet, but you can skip the main course and opt for the salad and dessert buffet, which features soup, salads, seafood, cold meats, cheese, pastries and fruit. After lunch, stroll around the beautiful gardens or sit beneath the palm trees enjoying the peaceful setting of one of the Gran Canaria's top hotels (▶ 43).

➕ 184 B2 ⊠ Hotel Maspalomas Oasis, Playa de Maspalomas
📞 928 141448 🕓 Daily 1–3 pm

PUERTO DE MOGÁN

La Bodeguilla Juananá £££

This chic little tavern on the harbourside square offers new Canarian cuisine from the German-Hungarian chef and his Canarian wife. They do everything with an artistic flourish, from the carved wooden seats to the big ceramic plates and the enormous handwritten menu boards brought to your table. The speciality is a selection of Canarian cheeses, served plain, steeped in olive oil or cooked in white wine. Other local ingredients turn up in unexpected ways, such as smoked swordfish with avocado followed by *gofio* ice-cream with palm honey for dessert. All of the wines served are Canarian.

➕ 178 B2 ⊠ Local 390 ☎ 928 565044 ⏰ Daily 7 pm–midnight

La Cofradía de Pescadores ££

The fishermen's cooperative by the harbour ought to have the freshest fish in town and it does not

disappoint. This is where the local fishermen gather during the day and it has a lively Spanish atmosphere, though it is popular with tourists as well. Most of the tables are outside on a bamboo-covered terrace with waterside views. Bread is served warm from the oven, with tomatoes, garlic and *allioli* (garlic mayonnaise). Grilled fish comes with a generous helping of vegetables.

➕ 178 B2 ⊠ Dársena Exterior del Puerto ☎ 928 565321 ⏰ Daily noon–11

ARGUINEGUÍN

La Cofradía ££

With checked tablecloths, fishing nets and posters of Atlantic fish on the walls, this simple harbourside restaurant is a reminder of the days when Arguineguín was little more than a fishing village. It is run by the fishermen's cooperative and situated at the end of a fish-packing warehouse. Local families come here at weekends and the

restaurant has built up a considerable reputation. There's fresh fish straight from the harbour, or paella, prawns or sole.

➕ 178 C1 ⊠ Puerto de Arguineguín ☎ 928 150963 ⏰ Daily 10 am–11 pm

PUERTO DE LA ALDEA

Aguas Marinas ££

With a handful of fish restaurants beside the harbour, Puerto de la Aldea has the feel of a working fishing village rather than a tourist resort. The fish here is likely to be fresh rather than frozen, especially if you ask for the catch of the day, simply grilled with salad and few spicy pototoes.

➕ 178 A4 ⊠ Calle Varadero 4 ☎ 928 891152 ⏰ Daily 11–11

PUERTO RICO

Bar La Parada £

This 24-hour, open-air tapas bar is about the only place in Puerto Rico

where you can expect to meet more locals than tourists. Buses and taxi drivers come here between shifts, timeshare salespeople meet up for breakfast, and clubbers stagger in for a final beer on their way home to bed. There is always a joint of roast pork on the bar, freshly carved into delicious sandwiches, as well as *tortilla* (potato omelette) and other tapas. Most people stand at the counter, but there are a few tables on a terrace overlooking the park.

➕ 178 B2 ⊠ Calle Lanzarote (by the bus stop) ⏰ 24 hours

La Cantina ££–£££

The owner has amassed a huge selection of wines from all over Spain and beyond. This is mostly a place to meet before dinner for a glass of champagne or sherry and a plate of ham, cheese or *foie gras*, but they also do prime grilled steaks and fondues. Make sure to take a look at the impressive wine cellar.

➕ 178 B1 ⊠ Apartamentos El Greco, Calle Doreste y Molina

☎ 928 560040 ⓖ Wed–Mon
6 pm–3 am (last orders 11.30 pm)

Gran Canaria ££

Most of the places along the promenade offer menus with barbecued meat and fish and a beachfront atmosphere. This one feels more like a real restaurant, sheltered under an awning. It has the reputation of serving the biggest steaks in Puerto Rico. Desserts come with flaming sparklers.

✚ 178 B1 ☒ Playa de Puerto Rico
☎ 928 561354 ⓖ 10 am–11 pm

El Tiburón ££

The stroll along the promenade is an evening ritual in Puerto Rico, as waiters outside each restaurant vie for your attention with free glasses of sangría and promises of serving the freshest fish. This restaurant, whose name means "the shark", offers a good menu of fresh fish and excellent pizzas.

✚ 178 B1 ☒ Playa de Puerto Rico
☎ 928 560227 ⓖ 10 am–11 pm

Where to...
Shop

SHOPPING CENTRES

Away from the beach, resort life revolves around the *centros comerciales* – shopping centres by day and entertainment centres at night. These massive emporia have supermarkets, souvenir shops and news-stands as well as numerous shops selling alcohol, tobacco, perfume, electronics, cameras, watches and leather at duty-free prices. The quality is not always high, but prices are often negotiable and there are genuine bargains to be had if you shop around.

Playa del Inglés alone has around 13 shopping centres. The biggest, Cita, has more than 200 shops with an abundance of jewellery, leather, shoes and designer clothes. Look out for Aqua Marina (jewellery), Candle Palaco (gift candles), Lacoste (fashions), Macy's (sportswear) and Melilla (leather).

Among the more upmarket centres are Faro 2 at Maspalomas, with branches of Benetton, Lacoste, Armand Basi and Lladro porcelain, and the Anfi Centre at Anfi del Mar, an indoor mall with chic fashion boutiques and craft shops.

ARTS AND CRAFTS

Fedac, inside the tourist information office at Playa del Inglés, is a government-sponsored craft shop selling Canarian handicrafts, such as pottery, lace and musical instruments. Prices are fixed but the quality is guaranteed and as the shop does not make a profit you know that your money is going direct to the producer.

Juanana, on the harbourside at Puerto de Mogán, is a quirky *bodega* (wine shop) and craft shop where you can buy Canarian wines and cheeses as well as local artwork and ceramics. Also on the water-front in Puerto de Mogán, Rincon Canario has a more conventional range of souvenirs including pottery, jewellery and Guanche-style crafts.

In.and, there are craft shops in the village of Fataga and also in Ingenio, where the Museo de Pied-as y Artesania Canaria has embroidery and other crafts for sale.

MARKETS

The large weekly markets at Arguineguín (Tue), Puerto de Mogán (Fri) and San Fernando (Wed/Sat) are primarily designed for tourists, with a wide range of stalls selling leather, lace, inexpensive clothing and shoes, beachwear, beach towels, African carvings and drums at reasonable prices.

Although some of the stalls at these markets are "fixed price", at most stalls the initial asking price is inflated and you are expected to strike a bargain.

Where to...
Be Entertained

MUSIC AND DRAMA

To find out what's on in any particular area, check the listings in the newspapers or ask at the tourist offices in Puerto Rico, Maspalomas or Playa del Inglés. A good source of information and tickets is **AICTS** (tel: 928 769292; www.aicts.org), a non-profitmaking association which arranges trips to musical and operatic events in Maspalomas and Las Palmas.

Concerts are held at the Las Tirajanas Auditorium, which opened in 2000 inside the new convention centre at Las Meloneras.

Look out too for **open-air events**, including an Atlantic music festival on the beach at Playa del Inglés (Jan), a jazz festival in Puerto de Mogán (Feb) and a folk festival at Veneguera (Sep).

Agüimes

Agüimes is the venue for the **Encuentro Tres Continentes** (Three Continents Festival), which brings together theatre groups from Europe, Africa and America for a feast of drama and street theatre each September.

The same town also hosts an annual festival of Spanish and Latin American storytellers in January.

NIGHTLIFE

For many visitors, the nightlife of the south coast resorts is one of the main reasons for a holiday in Gran Canaria.

Playa del Inglés

Most of the action takes place in the big shopping centres of Playa del Inglés, especially the area around the **Kasbah** and **Metro** centres.

The bars start to fill up early in the evening, reaching a peak at around midnight when most people move on to the all-night discos and clubs.

The **Cita** centre is another popular area, with large numbers of German bars and drag shows in the central plaza.

San Agustín

For serious late-night clubbers who want to keep going all night and into the morning, **La Roca** in San Agustín is an après-disco club which is open at weekends from 6 pm–1 am.

Gay nightlife

The focus of gay nightlife in Gran Canaria is the **Yumbo** centre in Playa del Inglés, which features more than 50 gay bars, clubs and saunas. During the day this is a family-oriented shopping centre, with buskers and portrait painters

In-House Entertainment

Much of the entertainment in the south of the island takes place in tourist hotels, with discos, karaoke nights, flamenco shows and children's activities.

Tour operators also lay on a wide range of daytime and evening entertainments, from camel safaris to champagne cruises and cabaret shows to Wild West nights.

There is very little that is authentically Spanish or Canarian about any of these, but if you don't mind letting your hair down with your fellow tourists, they can be good fun and children are usually well catered for.

Food and drink is often included in the price and audience participation is strongly encouraged.

doing brisk business, but after about 10 pm the gay character of the Yumbo starts to assert itself.

Casinos

Gran Canaria's second casino is inside the **Meliá Tamarindos Hotel** in San Agustín. Men are expected to wear a jacket and tie, and a passport is also required.

The casino is open daily 9 pm to 4 am. A number of tour operators arrange evening excursions to the casino, including a dinner show and cabaret.

FESTIVALS

Día de los Reyes (5 Jan): the eve of Epiphany is marked by a street parade in Agüimes, when the Three Wise Men distribute Christmas gifts to the children of the town.

Carnival (Feb): processions, masked dances and extravagant costumes on the streets of Agüimes and Playa del Inglés during the riotous build-up to Lent.

Día de las Islas Canarias (30 May): Canary Islands' Day is marked by expressions of popular culture, such as wrestling and folk-dancing displays. This is also the feast day of San Fernando, a suburb of Playa del Inglés.

San Antonio de Padua (weekend before 13 Jun): a traditional pilgrimage in Puerto de Mogán in honour of the patron saint, together with a folklore festival and religious processions.

La Virgen del Carmen (16 Jul): processions of fishing boats in Arguineguín, Puerto de Mogán and Puerto de la Aldea in honour of the Virgin Mary, the patron saint of fishermen.

San Antonio el Grande (first Sun in Aug): religious festival in Mogán, first held in the 1930s when a plague of locusts attacked the town.

Fiesta del Charco (10 Sep): one of the oldest celebrations on Gran Canaria. In the past the inhabitants of San Nicolás de Tolentino (▲ 144) would bathe naked in the *charco* (lagoon) at Puerto de la Aldea, but when this was banned by the church they took to wading in fully clothed, fishing with their bare hands and splashing each other with water. There is also a **Bajada de la Rama**, similar to that held in Puerto de las Nieves, in which villagers thrash the sea with branches in an effort to bring rain.

Nuestra Señora del Rosario (5 Oct): stick fights, plough-pulling contests, folk dancing, a battle of flowers and the scattering of water and *gofio* are all elements of this traditional festival in Agüimes (▲ 140).

Navidad (25 Dec): a popular nativity play is staged on Christmas evening at Veneguera.

OUTDOOR ACTIVITIES

Camel Trekking

Camel safaris are available in the Barranco de Fataga and the Maspalomas sand dunes. The main centres are La Baranda in the village of **Arteara** (tel: 928 798680), Molino del Agua at Fataga (tel: 928 172089) and Camello Safari Dunas at **Maspalomas** (tel: 928 772058). Several tour operators offer camel-trekking excursions, usually combined with a meal at a ranch or tea in a Berber-style tent.

Cycling

Bicycles can be hired in all of the main resorts. Touring bikes, mountain bikes, rollerblades and helmets are all available from **Happy Biking** (Hotel Continental, Avenida de Italia 2, Playa del Inglés, tel: 928 766832.

Fishing

Deep-sea fishing trips depart from the harbour at Puerto Rico (▲ 142). Most trips leave at around 9 am, returning at 3 pm, though some operators also offer sunset trips. Advance booking is essential.

Fishing is also possible in the Soria reservoir in the Barranco de

Arguineguin, though you will need a licence (enquire at your nearest tourist office).

Go-karting

The **Gran Karting Club** at San Agustin claims to be the largest in Europe, with separate tracks for adults, teenagers and young children (on the C812 at Tarajalillo, just outside San Agustin on the road to Las Palmas, tel: 928 157190, open daily 10–9, expensive).

Golf

The oldest established golf course in the south is at **Maspalomas** (tel: 928 762581).

This 18-hole course is on the edge of the dunes and facilities include club rental, driving range, putting green and restaurant. A second course opened in 2000 at **El Salobre** (tel: 828 061828), off the GC1 motorway near Arguineguin. New courses are under construction at Las Meloneras and Tauro and are scheduled to be open by 2002.

Horse-riding

Riding lessons and excursions are available at **Rancho Park** on the road to Palmitos Parque (tel: 928 766874)

Rancho Grande in Juan Grande (tel: 928 728115), which also offers moonlit rides and pony rides for younger children.

Jeep safaris

Tour operators in the resorts offer jeep safaris in the mountains, travelling through the *barrancos* (gorges) in a convoy of off-road vehicles. You are not usually expected to drive but whether you are a driver or a passenger, it is important to check that you have adequate insurance. If you don't want to hire a car, this is a memorable way to experience some of Gran Canaria's most dramatic scenery. Be prepared to get dirty, dusty and hot.

Book through **Zig-Zags Safari**, Avenida de Italia 164, Playa del Inglés, tel: 928 776459, expensive.

Tennis and squash

A number of hotels have their own tennis courts. There are public tennis and squash courts at the Maspalomas golf course and in the park beside the bus stop at Puerto Rico.

Walking

Guided walks in the mountains are offered by **Rutas Canarias** (tel: 689 775034), with minibus transfers to and from Playa del Inglés. You need to meet outside the tourist office at the Yumbo centre at 10 am on Monday, Wednesday or Friday, returning at around 6 pm. Take good shoes, water and a picnic.

Another company offering a varied programme of guided walks is **Viajes Las Palomas** (tel: 928 764195), inside the shopping centre at San Agustin.

Watersports

Windsurfing, sailing, jet-skiing and diving are available at all of the main resorts.

Experienced **windsurfers** should head for Pozo Izquierdo on the southeast coast or Playa del Águila at San Agustin, where the family of former world champion Björn Dunkerbeck runs a windsurfing school (tel: 928 762958).

Scuba diving courses can be booked with Canary Diving Adventures at Playa de Taurito (tel: 928 565428). Aquanauts at Puerto Rico (tel: 928 560655) and Scubasur at Anfi del Mar (tel: 928 150105).

Beginners will learn in swimming pools and sheltered harbours, but for experienced divers the top location is the lava reef off Pasito Blanco, where there are schools of grouper and moray eels.

Parascending, which involves flying up to 200m in a parachute while attached to a boat, is available at Puerto Rico and Playa del Inglés. This is an expensive thrill, but like many of these activities, it is sometimes available at a discount when combined with a boat trip.

Walks & Drives

1 LAS PALMAS
Walk

This gentle walk explores the old quarter of Las Palmas, with its historic houses, cobbled streets and shady squares. It's an ideal introduction for first-time visitors to the city, with visits to the cathedral, Columbus' house, Casa de Colón, and Museo Canario.

DISTANCE 3km **TIME** 1.5–2 hours
START POINT Parque San Telmo ⊞ 183 E3
END POINT Parque San Telmo ⊞ 183 E3

1–2
Leaving the bus station, walk across **Parque San Telmo** (➤ 67) with the military head-quarters in front of you, then turn left along **Calle Mayor de Triana** (➤ 67). This pedestrian shopping street begins close to the small chapel on the south side of the park. Walk along this promenade, admiring the mix of Modernist and neo-classical façades. Continue to the end of the street as it bends round to the left. Turn left to reach **Teatro Pérez Galdós**, the city's principal theatre. First opened in 1858, it burned down in 1918 and was rebuilt and named after the Canarian novelist. Outside the theatre, a bust of the French composer Camille Saint-Saëns recalls his visit to Gran Canaria.

2–3
Take care as you cross the busy highway which separates the district of Triana from Vegueta. Now you are approaching the oldest part of the city. On the far side of the road, look into the

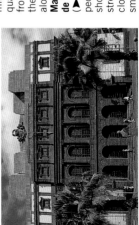

The Pérez Galdos theatre

Turn right along **Calle de los Balcones**, one of the prettiest streets in Las Palmas, with its typical Canarian houses and balconies. Note, on your right, the Casa de la Orden del Cachorro Canario (the Order of the Felt Hat), a society dedicated to Canarian culture. Also on this street is the **Centro Atlántico de Arte Moderno** (▶ 66), a modern art museum hiding behind an 18th-century façade.

4–5

Calle de los Balcones ends behind the cathedral in **Plaza del Pilar Nuevo**, dominated by the Biblioteca Colombina, a beautiful old house containing the library of the Casa de Colón. Turn left here across a leafy

Taking a Break

Of several pavement cafés on and around Plaza de Cairasco, the best spots are the **Alameda Café** and the terrace of the **Hotel Madrid** (▶ 41).

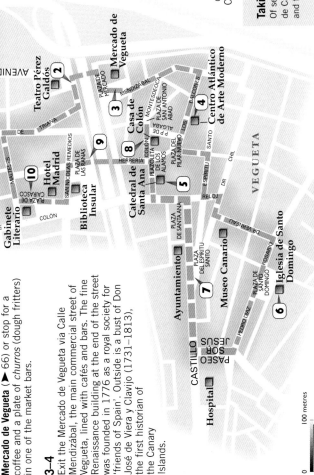

Mercado de Vegueta (▶ 66) or stop for a coffee and a plate of *churros* (dough fritters) in one of the market bars.

3–4

Exit the Mercado de Vegueta via Calle Mendizábal, the main commercial street of Vegueta, lined with cafés and bars. The fine Renaissance building at the end of the street was founded in 1776 as a royal society for 'friends of Spain'. Outside is a bust of Don José de Viera y Clavijo (1731–1813), the first historian of the Canary Islands.

Teatro Pérez Galdós ②

Gabinete Literario

Hotel Madrid ⑩

Biblioteca Insular ⑨

Mercado de Vegueta ③

Casa de Colón ⑧

Centro Atlántico de Arte Moderno ④

Catedral de Santa Ana ⑤

VEGUETA

Ayuntamiento

Museo Canario ⑦

Iglesia de Santo Domingo ⑥

Hospital

PASEO SOR JESUS

CASTILLO

0   100 metres
0   100 yards

square of bougainvillea, laurel and palm trees, then right into Calle Espíritu Santo. The entrance to the cathedral, **Catedral de Santa Ana** (▶ 60) is a short distance along this street on your right.

5–6

At the next junction, turn left along Calle Reloj and then right along Calle Dr Chil to reach the **Museo Canario** (▶ 56). Now go left

along Calle Dr Verneau, passing the museum entrance. Continue on this street for two blocks, then turn right along Calle Rosario into Plaza de Santo Domingo, a peaceful square with an 18th-century fountain at its centre. On Sunday mornings this is the venue for a busy **flower and craft market**, with music, dancing and activities for children. The church of Santo Domingo dates from the 16th century and contains an altarpiece by the Canarian artist Luján Pérez.

6–7

Leave the square in the northwest corner along Calle Pedro Díaz, climbing gently towards Paseo Sor Jesús. Turn right here along the walls of an old hospital and right again along Calle Castillo, where there

Pause for a rest during your walk in the leafy gardens of Plaza del Espíritu Santo

are several fine old Canarian houses. As you walk down this street, there are good views of the Catedral Santa Ana ahead. The street ends in **Plaza del Espíritu Santo**, one of Vegueta's most charming spaces, with a covered fountain set in its own small garden and a stately palm tree. The chapel dates from 1615 and has a revered image of Christ which is used in the city's Good Friday processions. The house next to the church was the home of Silvestre de Balboa, born in Las Palmas in 1563 and author of the first known work of Cuban literature.

7–8

From Plaza del Espíritu Santo it is just a few steps downhill to **Plaza de Santa Ana**, once the city's main square. The square is surrounded by flat-roofed Renaissance mansions containing, among others, the episcopal palace and the residence of the former governors. Bronze dogs, symbols of the Canary Islands, stand guard at the far end of the square. The best place to take it all in is from a vantage point on the steps of the old town hall, facing the Catedral Santa Ana. Turn left in front of the cathedral and take the next right to reach **Plazoleta de los Álamos**. Directly in front of you as you enter this small square is the façade of the **Casa de Colón** (▶ 63), with its carved stone doorway, wooden balconies, gargoyles and coat of arms. Keep straight on along Calle Colón to reach the entrance to the house.

8–9

Just beyond the Casa de Colón, **Plaza de San Antonio Abad** marks the origins of the city. It was here that Juan Rejón founded the city in 1478 – there's a plaque on the wall in Pasaje Pedro de Algaba. The small chapel here was the first church in Las Palmas, where Columbus is said to have prayed for the success of his voyages to America. Retrace your steps along Calle Colon and turn right down Calle Herrería to return to the highway, built on the site of the Guiniguada ravine. Cross the road to reach **Plaza de las Ranas**, named after the frogs which used to live in the stream. The area around the Boulevard Monopol shopping mall is now a popular night haunt.

9–10

Turn left just beyond the library to reach **Plaza de Cairasco**. This triangular square is perhaps the most emblematic of all Las Palmas' open spaces. At the centre is a fountain and a bust of Bartolomé Cairasco, a 16th-century Canarian poet. To the right is the Hotel

Madrid, where Franco spent the night before launching his military rebellion in 1936. The **Gabinete Literario**, dominating the square, is Las Palmas' finest 19th-century building, with neo-classical and Modernist touches. Founded in 1844, it is closed to visitors, but you can peer inside at the sumptuous entrance hall and grand staircase. Next to the square, **Alameda de Colón** is a stylish promenade with benches and a statue of Columbus (1892). Leave Plaza de Cairasco via Calle Malteses and retrace your steps along Cal le Mayor de Triana to Parque San Telmo.

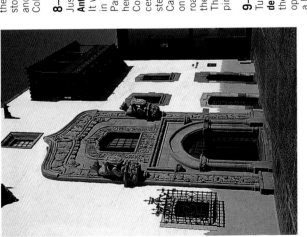

The monument to Bartolomé Cairasco in his eponymous square

The façade of the Casa de Colón

2 CRUZ DE TEJEDA
Walk

DISTANCE 4km **TIME** 1–1.5 hours
START POINT Cruz de Tejeda ⊞ 178 C4
END POINT Cruz de Tejeda ⊞ 178 C4

This short walk in the mountains gives spectacular views for the minimum of effort. It can easily be incorporated into the drive across the *cumbre* (▲ 161), or combined with a day-trip to Cruz de Tejeda and a hearty lunch.

1–2
Begin at **Cruz de Tejeda** (▲ 115) with the *parador* behind you and take the cobbled path to the right of Hotel El Refugio (▲ 43). When the path divides, keep to the left fork, climbing between bushes of *retama* (broom) and *tajinaste* (viper's bugloss). The path ascends to a stone wall at the boundary of a fenced-off estate clearly marked with the sign "*Coto privado de ca*" ("No Hunting"). Keep straight ahead, following an **old donkey trail** along a ridge. Take your time admiring the sweeping panorama of the mountains. The landmarks of **Roque Nublo** (▲ 112) and **Roque Bentaiga** (▲ 110) are clearly visible in the foreground,

while Mount Teide on Tenerife appears on the horizon, usually floating on a sea of clouds. This is a wonderful place to watch the sunset.

2–3
Leaving the ridge, the path drops down between fences and pine trees towards a large pair of gates, then continues along a **grit track** between slopes planted with young pines. When the track swings round sharply to

On clear days Tenerife seems to actually float above the clouds

Taking a Break

There are cafés and snack stalls at **Cruz de Tejeda** and at the visitor centre at **Mirador de Becerra**. For a fuller meal, try **Yolanda** at Cruz de Tejeda (▶ 119).

out point on the old pilgrim route from San Mateo to San Bartolomé de Tirajana.

4–5

A path leads down to a **visitor centre** with exhibitions on the geology, environment and culture of the central mountains. There is a café here, and vans in the car-park sell drinks, ice-creams and souvenirs. After visiting the centre, return to **Cruz de Tejeda** by the same route. On a clear day the views stretch north as far as La Isleta in Las Palmas.

Places to Visit

Centro de Interpretación Degollada de Becerra

This interpretation centre is the result of a European Union initiative to promote rural tourism on Gran Canaria. Displays are captioned in Spanish but there is a booklet with English translations. A highlight is the panoramic observation window, with views across the mountain range and a panel to help you identify the various peaks.

✚ 180 B2 ☎ 928 170336 ⑩ Daily 10–5
⑫ Free

to the left, continue straight ahead by scrambling up on to a **path** where you are immediately rewarded with a magnificent view over the Barranco de la Mina. The houses of **Vega de San Mateo** (▶ 96), way down in the valley, sparkle in the distance.

3–4

The path now drops down to join a tarmac road. Turn right and keep to the road for around 200m, walking in the shade of tall Canary pine trees to your left and Canada pines to your right. When you see a **white house** on the right, leave the road to walk up the concrete driveway and follow the path to the left of the house. Keep to your left, passing a chestnut tree, and follow this mostly flagstoned path as it winds around the hillside, parallel to and above the road. When the path drops back down to the road, turn right to reach the **Mirador de Becerra**, a look-

3 COSTA CANARIA
Walk

DISTANCE 8km **TIME** 3 hours
START POINT San Agustín ✚ 185 E1
END POINT Faro de Maspalomas ✚ 184 B2

This delightful walk follows the Maspalomas coastline, also known as the Costa Canaria. On foot it is easy to appreciate the varied scenery of this stretch of coast, and the subtly differing character of the various resorts. With good bus connections to the start and finish, it's an easy day trip from any of the south coast resorts. The walk is mostly flat and can be done in good, comfortable sandals – apart from the dunes, which are best crossed barefoot.

1–2
Ask the bus driver to let you off at the **San Agustín roundabout**, then take the short road downhill to the **beach** at Maspalomas. Before you begin your walk, follow the beachside

The highlight of this walk is the trek across the Dunas de Maspalomas

promenade around to your left until it runs out. From here you have a good view of the entire walk, with the Faro de Maspalomas (lighthouse), your ultimate destination, visible beyond the sand dunes.

2–3

Retrace your steps along the **promenade** as it passes behind the beach and alongside the lush gardens of the Melia Tamarindos Hotel. The wide beach is rarely crowded and in the early morning it can be a very peaceful spot. After passing a small **lighthouse**, the path crosses the end of the beach beneath a row of pines and climbs on to a headland where it clings to the rocks between seafront bungalows and a series of rocky coves.

After a few minutes round the corner to see the large

back of the beach. As the path swings right towards the main road, continue straight ahead to cross the wooden footbridge at the mouth of a small *barranco* (gorge).

The bar on the bridge sells freshly squeezed juices of pineapple, guava, banana and cactus and makes an excellent place for a short rest.

Continue along the promenade for another five minutes to **Playa del Cochino**, a sheltered bay with sunloungers and a beach bar. Look out for the cactus garden of the Europalace Hotel to your right.

4–5

Now climb the steps to the Parque Tropical shopping centre which marks the start of **Playa del Inglés**. Take the left-hand path

3–4

Now the promenade drops back down to sea level to run along the

expanse of **Playa de las Burras** beneath you. This beach of golden sand, between San Agustín and Playa del Inglés, has a name which means "beach of the she-donkeys" in Spanish.

5–6

Take off your shoes and begin the long trek across the **dunes** towards the lighthouse. Make sure that you have plenty of water before you set out. As a rule, it is easier to weave in and out between the dunes than to attempt to take a direct path, as some of the dunes are up to 10m deep. The contours are constantly changing as the sand is sculpted by the wind. With the breeze against your face and hot sand between your toes, this is a real back-to-nature experience. It's worth noting that there can be nude sunbathing around here.

The walk across the dunes takes about an hour. Using the lighthouse to guide you, head towards Maspalomas beach, passing behind the lagoon to rejoin the crowds of bathers. Now walk along the beach until you come to the **Faro de Maspalomas** (lighthouse).

Buses to **San Agustín** and **Playa del Inglés** leave just inland from here. Alternatively, if you still have some energy, you can return to Playa del Inglés by walking along the shoreline (allow around 1.5 hours).

The end of the road for this walk is the lighthouse at Maspalomas, which you can use as a beacon to guide your way across the dunes

Taking a Break

There are numerous restaurants, bars and cafés in the **Parque Tropical shopping centre** (➤ 159) and behind the beach in **Playa del Inglés** (➤ 130).

around the shopping centre to rejoin the promenade, now wider and known as the **Paseo Costa Canaria**. Pine and bamboo trees cling to the slopes as you look down over the cliffs, with views of the Maspalomas sand dunes in the distance. The promenade gets busier as you approach the heart of the resort. Soon you reach a long flight of steps which leads down to the beach. Continue on the promenade high above the beach.

As the beach starts to widen, the path descends a steep staircase, crosses a road and climbs up again on the other side to leave the resort behind. Before long you are walking beside the dunes.

When the path finally runs out, follow the bend around to your right to reach a road, then turn left and walk through the archway of the **Riu Palace Maspalomas Hotel** (➤ 43) to arrive at the viewpoint overlooking the dunes.

4 ACROSS THE CUMBRE

Drive

DISTANCE 130km TIME 4 hours
START POINT Las Palmas 🔢 179 F5
END POINT Las Palmas 🔢 179 F5

This half-day drive across the sierra provides a vivid introduction to the diverse landscapes of the island. As the green, alpine north gives way to the harsh, arid south, it is easy to see why it is known as a continent in miniature.

1–2

Leave **Las Palmas** on the C811, following signs to Tafira. As you drive out of the city on this busy road, look up to admire the pastel-coloured houses of the *barrios* of **San Roque** and **San Juan**, clinging to the hillsides like some Cubist fantasy. The two-lane dual carriageway climbs steeply out of Las Palmas, passing the university and a water treatment plant. Shortly after the **Jardín Canario** (▶ 85), the road narrows to a single lane and runs through Tafira Alta. Continue through **Monte Lentiscal**, where much of Gran Canaria's wine is produced, to **Santa Brígida**. These prosperous villages have virtually become suburbs of

The houses of San Roque add an unexpected splash of colour

Las Palmas, where wealthy Canarios have homes away from the noise of the city.

2–3

Now the serious climbing begins. The road is shaded by tall pines and eucalyptus trees as it winds up towards **Vega de San Mateo** (▶ 96). The higher you go, the greener everything

becomes. The views are magnificent, but there are many twists and turns and you need to keep your eyes on the road. Eventually you reach **Cruz de Tejeda** (▶ 115), a good place to break your journey, with restaurants and cafés. If you want to stretch your legs, take the short walk from here to the **Mirador de Becerra** (▶ 1150).

3–4

The next section of the route is the most spectacular as you snake down towards the village of **Tejeda** (▶ 116). The monoliths of **Roque Bentaiga** (▶ 110) and **Roque Nublo** (▶ 112) loom dramatically. Continue on the C811, passing Roque Bentaiga on the way to **Ayacata**, a busy mountain crossroads with several restaurants and bars (▶ 114).

4–5

Drive through Ayacata, ignoring the turn-off to the right. The road now becomes the C815, signposted to San Bartolomé de Tirajana. There are fine views to your right over the Chira reservoir as you climb to the **Cruz Grande pass** (1,200m), which forms a natural barrier between north and south. The landscape visibly changes, becoming harsher and more rugged as you gaze down a series of gorges towards the south coast. Inland, the views are dominated by **Risco Blanco**, a huge wall of white rock.

The road continues to **San Bartolomé de Tirajana** (► 116), the small town at the head of the Barranco de Tirajana. (If you are staying on the south coast, you could complete the tour at this point and drive through the Barranco de Fataga to Playa del Inglés.)

Stay on the C815 as it passes through San Bartolomé and continue to the village of **Santa Lucía** (► 117).

Roque Bentaiga dominates the landscape

5–6

As you leave Santa Lucía, there is a fork in the road. Take the left fork, signposted to Las Palmas and Agüimes. At first the road climbs through a barren, rocky moonscape, but after 8km the village of **Temisas** appears as a cluster of white houses, surrounded by olive groves and clinging to the steep slopes of a gorge. Now the landscape grows greener once again, with more olive trees and cacti on the hillsides as you descend towards **Agüimes** (➤ 140).

The white-housed village of Temisas, surrounded by a rocky landscape, produces the best olives on Gran Canaria

Right: Take a detour along the Barranco de Guayadeque, where descendants of the original Guanches live in caves not much changed from earlier times

6–7

At the junction turn left to enter Agüimes, then left again to avoid the town. The road crosses the **Barranco de Guayadeque** (➤ 126). On the far side of the *barranco*, look back towards Agüimes to see the houses perched above the ravine. Next is **Ingenio**, a small town known for arts and crafts. At the traffic lights turn right into the one-way system towards a roundabout, where a monument of a sugar press recalls the town's history of sugar production. Take the last exit from the round-about to head back up the hill into Ingenio.

7–8

Reaching a crossroads, turn right onto the C816, following signs to Telde. The road passes the northern suburb of **Las Mejías** (which is home to a handicrafts museum) and crosses a rocky plateau with views of Gando Airport before descending to **Telde** (➤ 95). On entering Telde, turn right onto the ring road and follow signs to **Las Palmas** to return via the coastal motorway.

Taking a Break

For lunch try **Yolanda** at Cruz de Tejeda (➤ 119), **Viuda de Viera** at Ayacata (➤ 114) or **Hao** at Santa Lucía (➤ 1190).

AROUND THE ISLAND

Drive

This one-day drive follows the shoreline before heading inland into a fertile valley. It may seem a lot of ground to cover, but because of the fast motorways along the north and east coasts, it is possible. Along the way are all the different sides of Gran Canaria: mega-resorts, fishing villages and banana plantations as well as a testing stretch of coastal corniche.

DISTANCE 190km **TIME** 1 day
START POINT Puerto de Mogán ▐ 178 B2
END POINT Puerto de Mogán ▐ 178 B2

1–2

Begin in **Puerto de Mogán** (➤ 138) and head inland along the valley towards Mogán. After just over 1km, turn right to join the C812 coast road to Las Palmas. From here to Puerto Rico the road hugs the cliffs, passing a succession of bays and inlets which are slowly being taken over by tourism.

Shortly after the beach at **Playa de los Amadores** (➤ 143), you round a bend to see the apartment blocks of **Puerto Rico**

(➤ 142) climbing up the steep hillsides in front of you.

2–3

Continue on the coast road towards **Arguineguin** (➤ 141). Just beyond Arguineguin, bear

Puerto Rico is a popular centre for sailing and deep-sea fishing

right to stay on the C812. Passing a large banana plantation, turn right at the round-about to climb on to a headland overlooking a cement factory. Between here and Maspalomas there are numerous small beaches and coves. During the week this area is usually deserted and you can have an entire beach to yourself.

All this will change as this coastline is earmarked for further development, with new roads, golf courses and tourist villages stretching all the way from Maspalomas to Mogán. The yacht marina at **Pasito Blanco**, up until now an exclusive spot, will soon be connected to Maspalomas and the dunes by a seafront promenade.

3–4

Shortly after passing **Las Meloneras**, the road crests a hill and the conurbation of Playa del Inglés and Maspalomas is spread out beneath you. During the day, the **Dunas de Maspalomas**

(▲ 132) are visible to your right; at night, the lights of **Playa del Inglés** (▲ 129) sparkle below. Continue on the C812 as it passes through this area, skirting Playa del Inglés on its way to the neighbouring resort of **San Agustín** (▲ 122).

4–5

The road now hugs the coastline again on its way to **Juan Grande**. This ordinary looking village is the ancestral home of the Vega Grande family, responsible for much of the tourist development along the south coast. Just beyond Juan Grande, when the windmills of **Pozo Izquierdo** appear to your right, leave the C812 to join the GC1 motorway to Las Palmas.

5–6

The motorway now passes factories, shopping malls and Gando Airport on its way to Las Palmas. After bypassing **Telde**, it returns to the coast and as you round a bend **Playa de la Laja** comes into view. Now you are approaching the southern outskirts of Las Palmas.

As you enter the city, the motorway becomes the Avenida Marítima, bordered by a waterfront promenade popular with walkers and cyclists. Passing the yacht club, follow signs to Agaete and go through a tunnel to join the GC2.

6–7

You have now exchanged one motorway for another as you find yourself on the main road running along the north coast. As you emerge from the tunnel, look out for the **Auditorio Alfredo Kraus** to your right (▲ 70) behind the Las Arenas shopping centre at the end of **Playa de las Canteras** (▲ 70). The road now follows the coastline through a succession of small villages.

7–8

Just after **El Pagador**, where white houses jut out on a spit, the road climbs sharply to the **Puente da Silva**, a huge bridge high above a gorge. After more bridges and tunnels, the volcanic pyramid at **Gáldar** comes into view (▲ 98). Keep on the GC2 as it bypasses Gáldar towards **Agaete** (▲ 92). When the motorway runs out, turn right to **Puerto de las Nieves** (▲ 93), a good place to break your journey with a seafood lunch on the beach.

8–9

Take the road from Puerto de las Nieves to Agaete then turn right following signs to **San**

The windmills of Pozo Izquierdo

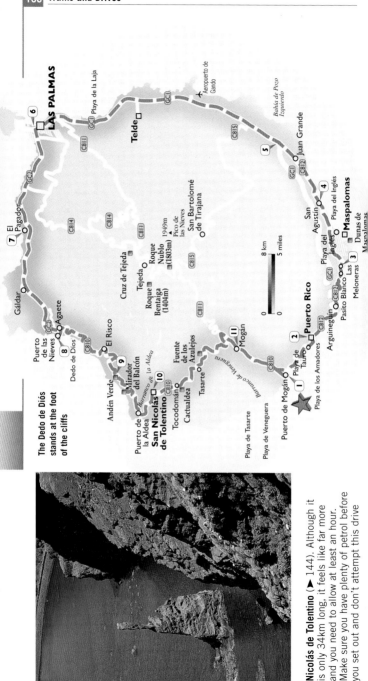

The Dedo de Diós stands at the foot of the cliffs

Nicolás de Tolentino (▶ 144). Although it is only 34km long, it feels like far more and you need to allow at least an hour. Make sure you have plenty of petrol before you set out and don't attempt this drive

The views from the spectacular Andén Verde coastal corniche stretch right along the northwest coast of the island, and if you're lucky you might even spot some dolphins basking in the sun

in difficult conditions, such as strong winds or heavy rain. The road climbs steeply into the hills and then sweeps around a gorge with views back down over Puerto de las Nieves and the **Dedo de Dios** (Finger of God) rock (➤ 93). The landscape here is very stark. Nothing grows on the hillsides except bushes of spiky *cardón* (euphorbia).

After passing a rocky outcrop, the road swings left, leaving the gorge behind. The cliffs drop sheer into the ocean beneath you. Eventually the road turns inland to reach the isolated settlement of **El Risco**, where a valley bed planted with gardens leads down to a remote and beautiful beach.

9–10

The views grow ever more dramatic as you approach the **Andén Verde** (➤ 93) coastal corniche, with Tenerife visible across the water and layer upon layer of volcanic cliffs receding into the distance.

As the road begins its slow descent into the plain of San Nicolás, pull into the well-marked parking area at the **Mirador del Balcón** to take in the views along the coast. The road now winds down the hillsides to the mouth of the **Barranco de la Aldea**. A short detour at this point leads to **Puerto de la Aldea**

(➤ 144), with its shingle beach, harbour and promenade.

Leaving the port, follow the C810 inland to the dusty town of **San Nicolás de Tolentino**,

(➤ 139). You are now heading inland, on a good road with numerous hairpin bends, **Tocodomán**, with the **Cactualdea Cactus Park** (➤ 139), makes a pleasant diversion and a chance to stretch your legs.

The C810 continues to climb into the foothills of the sierra. Signposts point the way down a series of valleys, to the remote west coast beaches of **Tasartico**, **Tasarte** and **Veneguera** (➤ 143). Roadside cafés advertise fresh papaya juice.

Shortly after the turn-off for Tasarte, you reach **Fuente de los Azulejos**, a remarkable multicoloured rock formation named after its resemblance to Portuguese tiles. It's worth getting out of the car here for a close-up look at this geological oddity. Passing the road to Veneguera and a turn-off leading to the high sierra (strictly for adventurous drivers!), the C810 now drops down to Mogán.

Follow the road through the town centre and continue along a fertile, well-populated valley to return to **Puerto de Mogán**, where you can have a cooling drink after a long day's drive in one of the harbour cafés

Unwind after your long drive with a stroll around the marina at Puerto de Mogán and check out some of the yachts

with the striking silhouette of **Roque Nublo** (➤ 112) visible on the skyline.

10–11

Reaching San Nicolás, turn right before a small windmill, following signs to **Mogán**

Taking a Break

Try **Las Nasas** at Puerto de las Nieves (➤ 100), a good seafood restaurant, or one of the many seafood places at Puerto de la Aldea.

Practicalities

Websites
- Spanish Tourist Board:
  www.tourspain.es
- Gran Canaria Info:
  www.gran-canaria-info.com

- Gran Canaria Tourist Board:
  www.idecnet.com/turismo
- Maspalomas Costa Canaria:
  www.maspalomas-web.org

In the UK
Spanish Tourist Office
22-23 Manchester Square
London W1M 5AP
☎ 020 7486 8077

BEFORE YOU GO

WHAT YOU NEED

		UK	Germany	USA	Canada	Australia	Ireland	Netherlands	Spain
●	Required								
○	Suggested								
▲	Not required								
△	Not applicable								
Passport/National Identity Card		●	●	●	●	●	●	●	▲
Visa		▲	▲	▲	▲	▲	▲	▲	▲
Onward or Return Ticket		○	○	●	▲	▲	○	○	○
Health Inoculations (tetanus and polio)		▲	▲	▲	▲	▲	▲	▲	△
Health Documentation (▶ 174, Health)		●	●	▲	▲	▲	●	●	
Travel Insurance		○	○	○	○	○	○	○	○
Driving Licence (national)		●	●	●	●	●	●	●	●
Car Insurance Certificate		●	●	●	●	●	●	●	○
Car Registration Document		●	●	●	●	●	●	●	○

WHEN TO GO

Gran Canaria

High season   Low season

JAN	FEB	MAR	APR	MAY	JUN	JUL	AUG	SEP	OCT	NOV	DEC
22°C	23°C	26°C	22°C	25°C	26°C	26°C	28°C	26°C	26°C	24°C	23°C

☀ Sun   ☁ Cloud   🌧 Wet   ⛅ Sun/Showers

The temperatures above are the **average daily maximum** for each month. Minimum temperatures rarely drop below 15°C; a year-round spring climate means that average temperatures range from 19°C in winter to 24°C in summer. On the south coast, which has over 300 days of sunshine a year, summer temperatures often exceed 30°C. The sea temperature varies from 19°C in January to 24°C in September. Most of the rain falls in the north, and there is occasional snow in the central mountains. The north is also affected by the *mar de nubes* "sea of clouds", low-lying clouds brought by the trade winds, and the *panza de burro* "donkey's belly", a grey haze which produces intense heat in summer. There is a second peak in July and August, when many Spanish families are on holiday. The quietest months are May, June, September and October.

In the USA
Tourist Office of Spain
666 Fifth Ave (35th Floor)
New York NY 10103
☎ 212 265 8822

Tourist Office of Spain
1221 Brickell Ave
Miami FL 33131
☎ 305 358 1992

For a complete list of
Spanish tourist offices
abroad, see
www.tourspain.es

GETTING THERE

By Air There are numerous charter flights to Las Palmas throughout the year from London and other European cities. Most seats are sold by tour operators as part of a package holiday, but it is usually possible to buy a flight-only deal through travel agents or on the internet. For independent travellers, the disadvantage of charter flights is that you are usually restricted to periods of 7 or 14 days.

The Spanish national airline, **Iberia**, has regular scheduled flights to Las Palmas via Madrid and Barcelona, with connections to major cities worldwide. From the USA, Canada, Australia and New Zealand, it is often cheaper to fly to London or Amsterdam and pick up a charter flight from there. Flight times are approximately four hours from London and two hours from Madrid.

By Sea The ferry company **Trasmediterránea** has a weekly car ferry service from Cádiz on the Spanish mainland to Tenerife and Gran Canaria. The journey from Cádiz to Las Palmas takes around 50 hours.

Inter-island Travel Binter Canarias has daily flights from Las Palmas to Tenerife and the other Canary islands. There are also regular ferry services from Las Palmas to ports in Fuerteventura, Lanzarote and Tenerife with connections to the other islands.

A high-speed jetfoil connects Las Palmas several times daily with Santa Cruz de Tenerife. The **Fred Olsen** line has six ferries a day from Puerto de las Nieves to Santa Cruz de Tenerife, with a journey time of one hour.

TIME

Unlike the rest of Spain, the Canary Islands observe Greenwich Mean Time (GMT). Summer time (GMT+1) operates from the last Sunday in March to the last Sunday in October.

CURRENCY AND FOREIGN EXCHANGE

Currency On 1 January 2002, the Euro replaced the peseta as the official currency of Spain. Pesetas will remain in circulation alongside the Euro for a period of six months and will cease to be legal tender in June 2002. Euro coins and notes are also legal tender in many other European countries, including France, Germany and Italy. Euro notes will be in denominations of 5, 10, 20, 50, 100, 200 and 500; coins will come in denominations of 1, 2, 5, 10, 20 and 50 cents.

Credit cards Major credit cards are widely accepted.

Exchange Banks generally offer the best rates for changing foreign currency and **travellers' cheques**, though money can also be changed at many travel agents, exchange bureaux and hotels. When changing travellers' cheques, you will need to show your passport. You can also withdraw cash from **ATM (cashpoint) machines** using your credit or debit card and a PIN (personal identification number). Your own bank will usually make a charge for this service.

TIME DIFFERENCES

| GMT 12 noon | Gran Canaria 12 noon | mainland Spain 1pm | Germany 1pm | USA (NY) 7am |

WHEN YOU ARE THERE

CLOTHING SIZES

UK	Rest of Europe	USA	
36	46	36	**Suits**
38	48	38	
40	50	40	
42	52	42	
44	54	44	
46	56	46	
7	41	8	**Shoes**
7.5	42	8.5	
8.5	43	9.5	
9.5	44	10.5	
10.5	45	11.5	
11	46	12	
14.5	37	14.5	**Shirts**
15	38	15	
15.5	39/40	15.5	
16	41	16	
16.5	42	16.5	
17	43	17	
8	34	6	**Dresses**
10	36	8	
12	38	10	
14	40	12	
16	42	14	
18	44	16	
4.5	38	6	**Shoes**
5	38	6.5	
5.5	39	7	
6	39	7.5	
6.5	40	8	
7	41	8.5	

NATIONAL HOLIDAYS

1 Jan	New Year's Day
6 Jan	Epiphany
19 Mar	St Joseph's Day
Mar/Apr	Good Friday, Easter Monday
1 May	Labour Day
30 May	Canary Islands' Day
May/June	Corpus Christi
15 Aug	Assumption of the Virgin
12 Oct	Spanish National Day
1 Nov	All Saints' Day
6 Dec	Constitution Day
8 Dec	Feast of the Immaculate Conception
25 Dec	Christmas Day

OPENING HOURS

○ Shops   ● Post Offices
● Offices   ◐ Museums
◐ Banks   ◐ Pharmacies

8am   9am   10am   noon   1pm   2pm   4pm   5pm   7pm

☐ Day   ▨ Midday   ☐ Evening

Shops The larger department stores in Las Palmas and many shops in the resorts stay open throughout the day. Most shops are closed on Sundays.
Banks Banks are closed on Sundays.
Restaurants Many restaurants in the larger resorts are open daily from around 10 am to midnight.
Museums and attractions Hours vary. As a general guideline they are open 10–1 and 4–8, but it is best to consult the individual times given for each sight in this guide.

POLICE 091

FIRE 080

AMBULANCE 061

PERSONAL SAFETY

Violence against tourists is unusual. Theft from cars is the most common form of crime, particularly in Las Palmas.

- Do not leave valuables on the beach or poolside.
- Always lock valuables in hotel safety deposit boxes.
- Never leave anything inside your car.
- Avoid the seamier streets in the port area of Las Palmas at night.

Police assistance:
 091 from any phone

TELEPHONES

There are public telephones on almost every street corner, with instructions in several languages. Most take coins, credit cards or phonecards (*tarjetas telefónicas*) which are available from post offices, kiosks and shops.

The cheap rate for international calls is 10 pm–8 am and all day Sunday.

International Dialling Codes
Dial 00 followed by

UK:	44
USA/Canada:	1
Ireland:	353
Australia:	61
Germany:	49

POST

Post boxes are yellow. The main post office in Las Palmas is at Avenida Primero de Mayo 62. Stamps (*sellos*) are available from post offices, hotels, news kiosks and tobacconists. A postcard to the UK or northern Europe will usually take about a week to arrive; allow 10–14 days to the USA.

ELECTRICITY

The power supply is 220 volts. Sockets take continental-style plugs with two round pins. Visitors from the UK will require an adaptor (often available at the airport) and visitors from the USA will require a voltage transformer.

TIPS/GRATUITIES

Tipping is not expected for all services, and rates are lower than in some countries. As a general guide:

Restaurants	5–10%
Cafés/bars	Discretion
Tour guides	Discretion
Taxis	10%
Hairdressers	10%
Chambermaids	10%
Porters	10%
Toilets	Discretion

CONSULATES and EMBASSIES

UK
☎ 928 262508

USA
☎ 928 271259

Ireland
☎ 922 245671

Germany
☎ 928 275700

France
☎ 928 292371

HEALTH

Insurance Citizens of the European Union and certain other countries receive free medical treatment in Spain with the relevant documentation (form E111 for UK nationals), although private medical insurance is still advised and is essential for all other visitors.

Dental Services Dental treatment has to be paid for by all visitors but is usually covered by private medical insurance.

Weather Visitors from cooler countries are especially vulnerable to the effects of the sun. You should cover up with a high-factor sunblock and drink plenty of non-alcoholic fluids. Children need to be well protected, especially when playing near the sea, as water and sand reflect the sun's rays.

Drugs Prescription and non-prescription drugs and medicines are available from pharmacies, usually distinguished by a large green cross. Outside normal hours, a notice on the door of each pharmacy should give the address of the nearest duty chemist.

Safe Water Tap water is generally safe to drink but has a high salt content. Mineral water is widely available and cheap, especially when bought at supermarkets in 5-litre containers.

CONCESSIONS

Students Gran Canaria and the other Canary Islands do not attract backpacking youngsters in the same way as other holiday islands and there are few student or youth concessions available. There are no youth hostels and only two official campsites on the island.

Senior Citizens Gran Canaria is an excellent destination for older travellers, especially in winter when the climate is clement. Some hotels and apartments offer long-stay discounts. The best deals are available through tour operators who specialise in holidays for senior citizens.

TRAVELLING WITH A DISABILITY

All new buildings in Spain have to be equipped with wheelchair access, but many older hotels, apartment blocks and public buildings are still inaccessible. Some buses have doors which lower to ground level for wheelchair access. Before booking a holiday, you should discuss your particular needs with your tour operator or hotel.

CHILDREN

Hotels and restaurants are generally very child friendly, and many hotels have playgrounds, parks, mini-golf and children's pools. Some tour operators also provide children's clubs and activities as part of your holiday. However, facilities such as baby-changing rooms are rare.

TOILETS

There are public toilets in shopping centres and at some larger beaches. Other useful standbys are department stores, museums and bars.

CUSTOMS

The import of wildlife souvenirs sourced from rare or endangered species may be either illegal or require a special permit. Before buying, check your home country's customs regulations.

SURVIVAL PHRASES

Yes/no **Sí/no**
Please **Por favor**
Thank you **Gracias**
You're welcome **De nada**
Hello **Hola**
Goodbye **Adiós**
Good morning **Buenos días**
Good afternoon **Buenas tardes**
Good night **Buenas noches**
How are you? **¿Qué tal?**
How much is this? **¿Cuánto vale?**
I'm sorry **Lo siento**
Excuse me **Perdone**
I'd like **Me gustaría…**
Open **Abierto**
Closed **Cerrado**

Today **Hoy**
Tomorrow **Mañana**
Yesterday **Ayer**
Monday **Lunes**
Tuesday **Martes**
Wednesday **Miércoles**
Thursday **Jueves**
Friday **Viernes**
Saturday **Sábado**
Sunday **Domingo**

DIRECTIONS

I'm lost **Me he perdido**
Where is…? **¿Dónde está?**
How do I get to…?
   ¿Cómo se va…?
   the bank **al banco**
   the post office
   a la oficina de correos
   the train station
   a la estación de trenes

Where are the toilets?
   ¿Dónde están los servicios?
Left **a la izquierda**
Right **a la derecha**
Straight on **todo recto**
At the corner **en la esquina**
At the traffic-light **en el semáforo**
At the crossroads **en la intersección**

IF YOU NEED HELP

Help! **¡Socorro! / ¡Ayuda!**
Could you help me, please
   ¿Podría ayudarme, por favor?
Do you speak English? **¿Habla inglés?**
I don't understand **No comprendo**
I don't speak Spanish
   No hablo español
Could you call a doctor?
   **¿Podría llamar a un médico,
   por favor?**

ACCOMMODATION

Do you have a single/double room?
   **¿Le queda alguna habitación
   individual/doble?**
   with/without bath/toilet/shower
   **con/sin baño propio/
   lavabo propio/ducha propia**
Does that include breakfast?
   ¿Incluye desayuno?
Could I see the room?
   ¿Puedo ver la habitación?
I'll take this room
   Me quedo con esta habitación
The key to room…, please
   **La llave de la habitación…,
   por favor**
Thank you for your hospitality
   Muchas gracias por la hospitalidad

NUMBERS

1	**uno**	11	**once**	21	**veintiuno**	200	**doscientos**
2	**dos**	12	**doce**	22	**veintidós**	300	**trescientos**
3	**tres**	13	**trece**	30	**treinta**	400	**cuatrocientos**
4	**cuatro**	14	**catorce**	40	**cuarenta**	500	**quinientos**
5	**cinco**	15	**quince**	50	**cincuenta**	600	**seiscientos**
6	**seis**	16	**dieciséis**	60	**sesenta**	700	**setecientos**
7	**siete**	17	**diecisiete**	70	**setenta**	800	**ochocientos**
8	**ocho**	18	**dieciocho**	80	**ochenta**	900	**novecientos**
9	**nueve**	19	**diecinueve**	90	**noventa**	1000	**mil**
10	**diez**	20	**veinte**	100	**cien**		

RESTAURANT

I'd like to book a table
   ¿Me gustaría reservar una mesa?
Have you got a table for two, please
   **¿Tienen una mesa para dos
   personas, por favor?**
Could we see the menu, please?
   ¿Nos podría traer la carta, por favor?
Could I have the bill, please?
   ¿La cuenta, por favor?
service charge included
   servicio incluido

breakfast **el desayuno**
lunch **el almuerzo**
dinner **la cena**
table **una mesa**
waiter/waitress **camarero/camarera**
starters **los entremeses**
main course **el plato principal**
dessert **postres**
dish of the day **plato del día**
bill **la cuenta**

MENU READER

aceituna olive
ajo garlic
alcachofa
   artichoke
almejas clams
almendras
   almonds
anguila eel
arroz rice
atún/bonito tuna

bacalao cod
berenjena
   aubergine
biftec steak
bocadillo sandwich
boquerones
   anchovies

calamares squid
caldo broth
callos tripe
cangrejo crab
cebolla onion
cerdo pork
cerezas cherries
cerveza beer
champiñones
   mushrooms
chorizo spicy
   sausage
chuleta chop
churros fritters
ciruela plum
cochinillo asado
   roast suckling
   pig
codorniz quail
conejo rabbit
cordero lamb

crema cream
criadillas
   sweetbreads
crudo raw

endibia chicory
ensalada (mixta)
   mixed salad
ensaladilla rusa
   Russian salad
espárragos
   asparagus
espinaca spinach

fideos noodles
filete fillet
flan crème
   caramel
frambuesa
   raspberry
fresa strawberry
**fruta (de
temporade)**
   seasonal fruit

galleta biscuit
gambas prawns
garbanzos
   chickpeas
gazpacho andaluz
   gazpacho (cold
   soup)
grosellas red/black
   currants
guisantes peas

habas broad beans
helado ice-cream
hígado de oca
   goose liver

**huevos fritos/
   revueltos**
   fried/scrambled
   eggs

jamón ham
judías verdes
   French beans
jugo fruit juice

langosta lobster
langostino
   crayfish
leche milk
lechuga lettuce
legumbres
   vegetables
lengua tongue
lenguado sole
liebre hare
lomo de cerdo
   pork tenerloin

manzana apple
mariscos seafood
mejillones
   mussels
melocotón peach
melón melon
merluza hake
mero sea bass
morcilla black
   pudding

pan bread
pato duck
pepino cucumber
pepinillos
   gherkins
pera pear

perdiz partridge
perejil parsely
pez espada
   swordfish
pescado fish
pimientos red/
   green peppers
piña pineapple
plátano banana
pollo chicken
puerro leek
pulpo octopus

queso cheese

rape monkfish
riñones kidneys
rodaballo turbot

salchicha sausage
salchichón salami
salmón salmon
salmonete red
   mullet
solomillo de buey
   fillet of beef
sopa soup

tocino bacon
tortilla española
   Spanish
   omelette
tortilla francesa
   plain omelette
trucha trout

verduras green
   vegetables

zanahorias carrots

Atlas

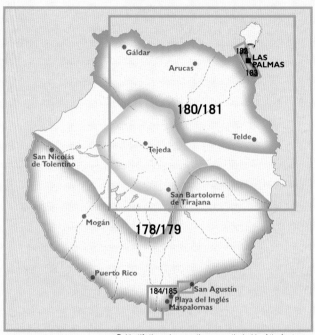

Gáldar

Arucas

182 **LAS PALMAS**

183

180/181

Telde

San Nicolás de Tolentino

Tejeda

San Bartolomé de Tirajana

Mogán

178/179

Puerto Rico

184/185 San Agustín

Playa del Inglés

Maspalomas

To identify the regions, see the map on the inside of the front cover

Regional Maps

━━━	Major route	☐	City
═══	Motorway	▫	Town
▪▪▪	Main road	o o	Village
-----	Other road	▣	Featured place of interest
✈	Airport	▪	Place of interest

Streetplans

▦	Important building	▣	Featured place of interest

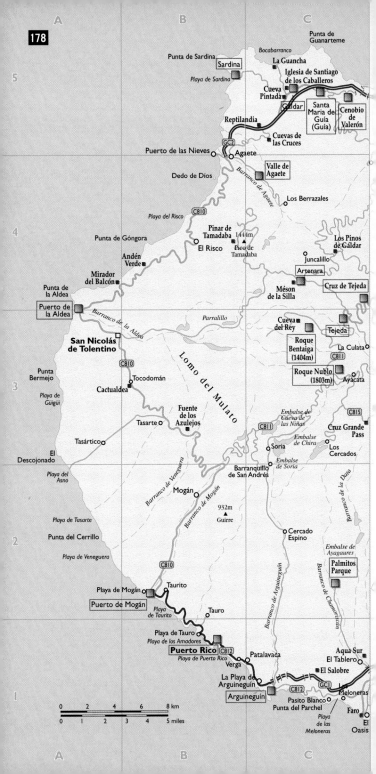

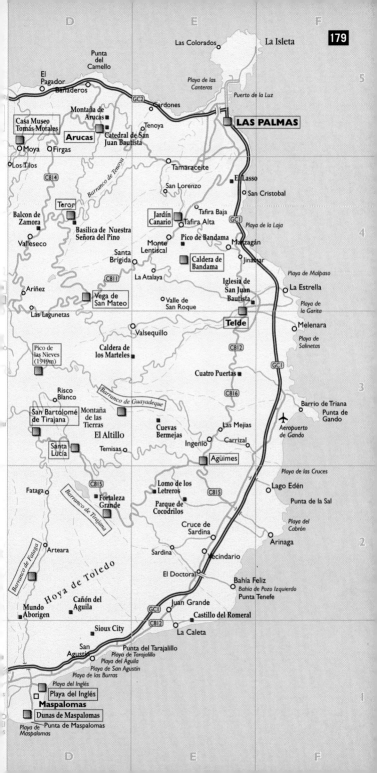

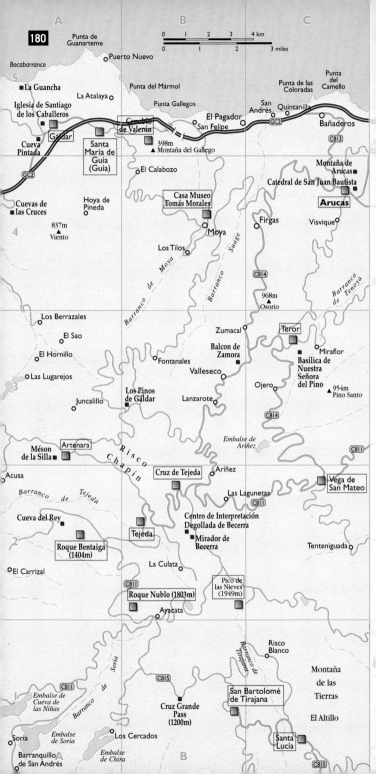

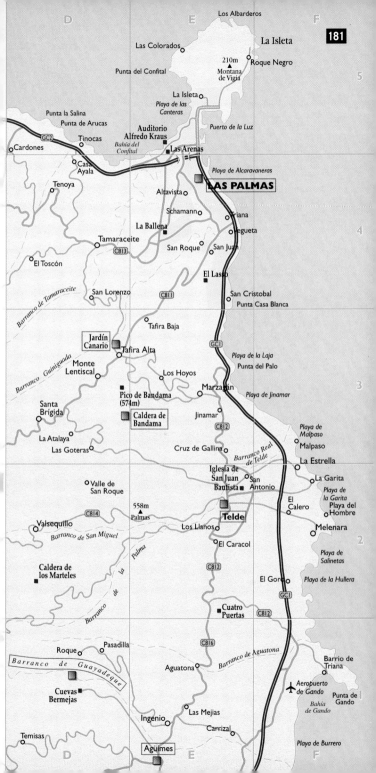

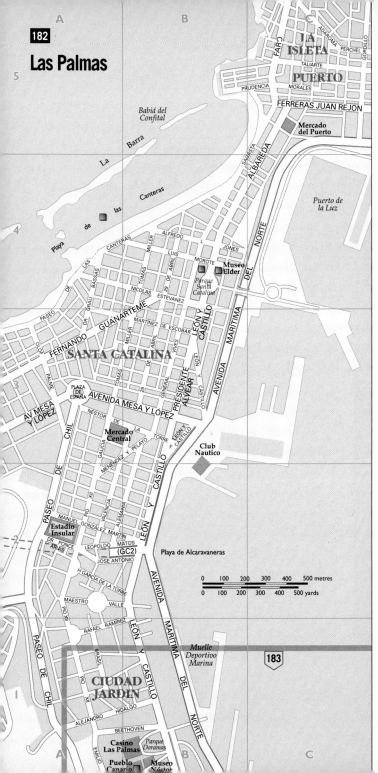

Las Palmas

LA ISLETA

FARO

ADÁRGOMA

PERCHEL

GORDILLO

TALIARTE

PUERTO

PRUDENCIA

MORALES

FERRERAS JUAN REJÓN

Babiá del Confital

Mercado del Puerto

La

Barra

SAGASTA

ALBAREDA

Puerto de la Luz

Canteras

DEL

NORTE

las

ALFREDO

JONES

Playa

de

CANTERAS

MILLER

LUIS

de

LAS

BASSAS

TOMAS

29 DE ABRIL

MOROTE

Museo Elder

NICOLAS

ESTEVANEZ

Parque Santa Catalina

DR GRAU

PASEO

GUANARTEME

MARTÍNEZ DE ESCOBAR

LEÓN Y CASTILLO

AVENIDA

MARÍTIMA

FERNANDO

MILLER

29

TOMAS

IVES

GENERAL

NOEL

PRESIDENTE ALVEAR

CASTILLO

OLOF

PALME

SANTA CATALINA

PLAZA DE ESPAÑA

AVENIDA MESA Y LÓPEZ

AV MESA Y LÓPEZ

CHIL

NÉSTOR

DE

LA

TORRE

LEÓN Y CASTILLO

DE

GALICIA

Mercado Central

MENÉNDEZ Y PELAYO

Club Nautico

PASEO

PIO XII

VALENCIA

ALEMANIA

LEÓN Y CASTILLO

MANUEL GONZÁLEZ MARTÍN

Estadio Insular

DR PONCE

ARIAS

LEOPOLDO MATOS

(GC2)

JOSE ANTONIO

Playa de Alcaravaneras

H GARCIA DE LA TORRE

MAESTRO VALLE

0	100	200	300	400	500 metres
0	100	200	300	400	500 yards

PIO XII

RAFAEL RAMÍREZ

LEÓN Y CASTILLO

AVENIDA

MARÍTIMA

DEL

NORTE

Muelle Deportivo Marina

183

PASEO DE CHIL

BRASIL

PIO XII

CIUDAD JARDÍN

HIDALGO

ALEJANDRO

BEETHOVEN

EMILIO

Casino Las Palmas

Parque Doramas

Pueblo Canario

Museo Néstor

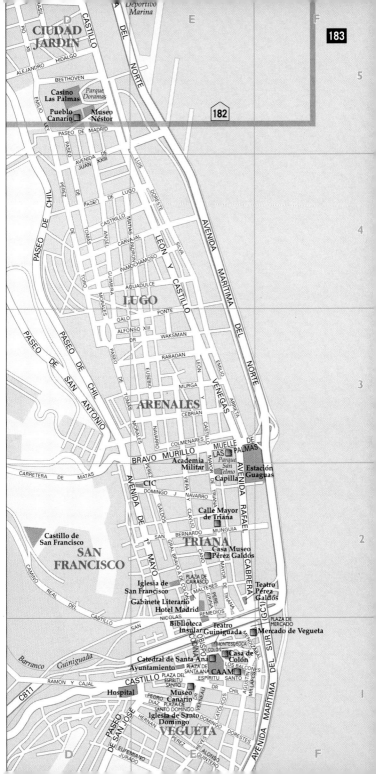

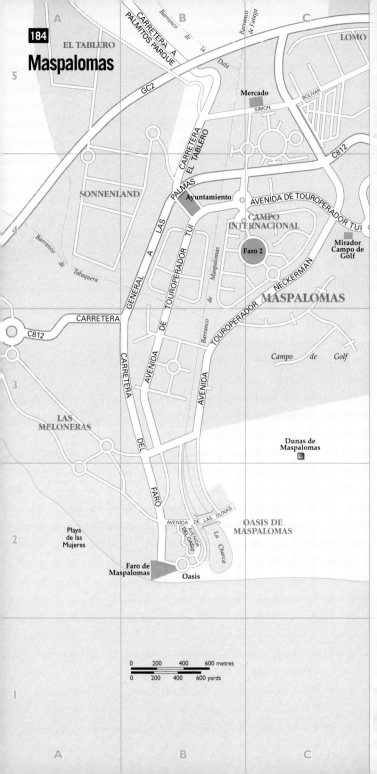

Playa del Inglés

San Agustín →

SAN FERNANDO

GC2

C812

CARRETERA GENERAL A LAS PALMAS

AVENIDA DE GALDAR

TIRAJANA

AVENIDA DE

AVENIDA

AVENIDA DE

ALFERECES

Yumbo

AVENIDA DE ESTADOS UNIDOS

AV. DE GRAN CANARIA

AVENIDA DE TIRAJANA

AVENIDA DE ESPAÑA

SARGENTOS

AVENIDA

AVENIDA DE GRAN TENERIFE

DE

PROVISIONALES

Kasbah Metro

Plaza de Maspalomas

PROVISIONALES

AVENIDA CANARIA

AVENIDA

DE ITALIA

PASEO COSTA

PASEO MADRID

Parque Tropical

Playa del Cochino

DE BONN

AVENIDA INGLATERRA

DE ALEMANIA

Cita

AV. DE FRANCIA

DE DINAMARCA

AVENIDA FINLANDIA

PASEO COSTA

AVENIDA CANARIA

PLAYA DEL INGLÉS

San Agustín

Sioux City (Cañon del Aguila)

GC2

SAN AGUSTÍN

C812

LOS GIRASOLES

LOS CLAVELES

Barranco del Toro

LOS PINOS

← Playa del Inglés

CARRETERA GENERAL A LAS PALMAS

LAS MARGARITAS

LAS RETAMAS

LAS ACACIAS

LOS JAZMINES

Playa de Morro Besudo

LAS

Faro

Playa de San Agustín

Playa de las Burras

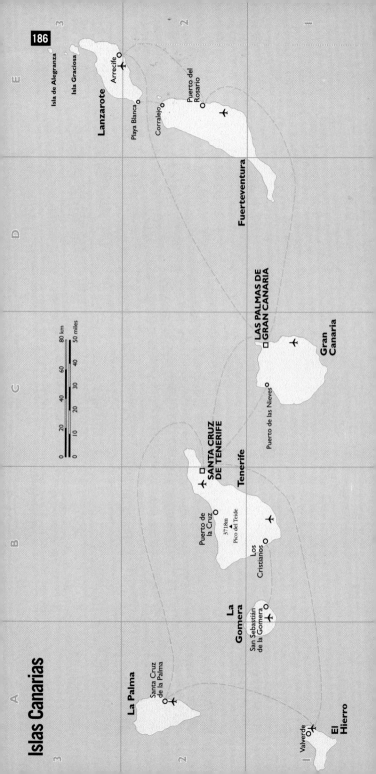

Islas Canarias

La Palma

Santa Cruz de la Palma

La Gomera

San Sebastián de la Gomera

El Hierro

Valverde

Tenerife

SANTA CRUZ DE TENERIFE

Puerto de la Cruz

3718m Pico del Teide

Los Cristianos

Gran Canaria

LAS PALMAS DE GRAN CANARIA

Puerto de las Nieves

Fuerteventura

Corralejo

Puerto del Rosario

Playa Blanca

Lanzarote

Arrecife

Isla Graciosa

Isla de Alegranza

0 20 40 60 80 km

0 10 20 30 40 50 miles

Picture credits

The Automobile Association wishes to thank the following photographers and libraries for
their assistance in the preparation of this book.

Front and Back Covers (t) AA Photo Library/Clive Sawyer; (ct) AA Photo Library/JA Tims;
(cb) AA Photo Library/JA Tims; (b) AA Photo Library/JA Tims
Spine AA Photo Library/JA Tims

ART DIRECTORS AND TRIP PHOTO LIBRARY 28b (A Tovy); HULTON ARCHIVE 7b,
MARY EVANS PICTURE LIBRARY 7t, 64t, EYE UBIQUITOUS 82/3, JAMES DAVIS WORLD-
WIDE 3i, 21t, 28t, 121; PAUL MURPHY 83, 136c, PICTURES COLOUR LIBRARY 8/9, 10/11,
16b, 21b, 32, 116, 122, ROBERT HARDING PICTURE LIBRARY 109, TOPHAM PICTURE-
POINT 8/9t, 26/7, THE TRAVEL LIBRARY 2iv, 3i, 20c, 77, 78 (S Black), 94, 103 (S Black),
104 (S Black), 124b (Philip Enticknapp), 134/5, 138/9, 142 (Philip Enticknapp); WORLD
PICTURES 21c, 29, 30.

The remaining photographs are held in the Association's own library and were taken by Pete
Bennett, with the exception of 2i, 2ii, 5, 12, 20b, 22t, 23b, 32/3, 33b, 35, 52, 79, 80b, 81b, 87,
92, 110, 113, 124c, 131, 137, 138, 152, 163r, 166 which were taken by Clive Sawyer and 11b,
13t, 13b, 15, 23t, 24c, 31c, 84, 85l, 86, 90/1, 98, 106c, 106b, 108, 109/9, 117, 118, 132/3, 141,
143, 144, 158, 163l, 167, 173t, 173cl, 173cr which were taken by James Tims.

Abbreviations for terms appearing above: (t) top; (b) bottom; (l) left; (r) right; (c) centre

SPIRAL GUIDES

Questionnaire

Dear Traveler

Your comments, opinions and recommendations are very important to us. So please help us to improve our travel guides by taking a few minutes to complete this simple questionnaire.

Send to: Spiral Guides, MailStop 66, 1000 AAA Drive, Heathrow, FL 32746–5063

Your recommendations…
We always encourage readers' recommendations for restaurants, nightlife or shopping – if your recommendation is added to the next edition of the guide, we will send you a FREE AAA Spiral Guide of your choice. Please state below the establishment name, location and your reasons for recommending it.

_____

_____

_____

_____

_____

Please send me AAA Spiral_____
(see list of titles inside the back cover)

About this guide…
Which title did you buy?

_____ **AAA Spiral**

Where did you buy it? _____

When? m m / y y

Why did you choose a AAA Spiral Guide? _____

_____

_____

_____

Did this guide meet your expectations?

Exceeded ☐   Met all ☐   Met most ☐   Fell below ☐

Please give your reasons _____

_____

_____

_____

continued on next page…

Were there any aspects of this guide that you particularly liked?

_____

_____

_____

_____

_____

Is there anything we could have done better?

_____

_____

_____

_____

_____

About you...

Name (Mr/Mrs/Ms) _____

Address _____

_____

_____ **Zip** _____

Daytime tel nos. _____

Which age group are you in?

Under 25 ☐   25–34 ☐   35–44 ☐   45–54 ☐   55–64 ☐   65+ ☐

How many trips do you make a year?

Less than one ☐   One ☐   Two ☐   Three or more ☐

Are you a AAA member? Yes ☐   No ☐

Name of AAA club _____

About your trip...

When did you book? m m / y y   When did you travel? m m / y y

How long did you stay? _____

Was it for business or leisure? _____

Did you buy any other travel guides for your trip? ☐ Yes   ☐ No

If yes, which ones? _____

Thank you for taking the time to complete this questionnaire.